# Unvaccinated

## Our turn to talk

Elizabeth Hanson M. Ed.

# Book Info

Unvaccinated Our Turn to Talk

© Copyright 2022

Elizabeth Hanson M. Ed.

Cover Design by David Spring M. Ed.

Photo from Be Brave Washington

Published by Better Future Books

Ferndale, Washington

First Edition November 2022

For Updates and other versions, such as Epub, visit the book website: UnvaccinatedOurTurnToTalk.com

ISBN  978-1-7350048-3-9 (Softcover)

# Dedication

Dedicated to the unvaccinated and to those who have lost faith and trust in so many things since March of 2020, and to my husband, David Spring, without whom I wouldn't have been able to write this.

"Because the world is immensely complex, there are only two options for how to look at it. You can ignore the complexity and artificially simplify it into something easy to understand … or you can peer into it, discover that things are immensely complicated, and realize that at the end of the day it is very difficult to know anything with certainty. I would argue that (uncertainty) does not provide an excuse to claim ignorance on a subject; rather it creates an obligation to remain humble, look for holes in your belief system and be receptive to evidence that challenges your existing beliefs system."

- A Midwestern Doctor

# Primary Sources used for this book

1- The CDC

https://www.cdc.gov/nchs/nvss/vsrr/covid_weekly/index.htm#SexAndAge


2- Our World in Data

https://ourworldindata.org/coronavirus#explore-the-global-situation


3- Substack

https://substack.com


4- Worldometer

https://www.worldometers.info/


5- US Mortality

https://www.usmortality.com/


Note: There are links to more than one hundred additional sources listed by chapter in the Appendix

## About the Author

Elizabeth Hanson has a BA in Linguistics from the University of Washington and an M.Ed. in Adult Education from Temple University. She worked as a nursing assistant for 7 years while going to school.

Elizabeth has taught English to people born in other countries (ESL) since 1985 and taught at Shoreline Community College, located just north of Seattle, Washington from 1992-2021.

Elizabeth's knowledge of science comes from taking the required science courses in high school and college. She learned basic human anatomy and physiology by co-writing a book with a biologist entitled **Anatomy and Physiology for English Language Learners** (2006).

Elizabeth's passion for many years was helping English language students prepare for the science courses they needed to take before entering nursing and other healthcare related programs. She co-designed and co-taught two pre-college level courses for English language students: **Medical Terminology** and **Anatomy and Physiology.** She learned a great deal from the biologist and medical terminologist with whom she worked.

Having a keen interest in health helped her understand the scientific research as she has read about Covid nearly every day since March 2020. This book is the result of that research.

# CONTENTS

# Preface

As of August 13th 2022, 67% of people in the US were fully vaccinated against SARS-CoV-2, the formal term for the corona virus that has caused both an economic and psychological upheaval in the US and much of the world. (When I say fully vaccinated, in this book I mean that they took the initial 2 Pfizer of Moderna vaccines or the one Johnson & Johnson vaccine.)

Many people in the US are forced to be fully vaccinated in order to keep their jobs, serve in the US military or to attend college or university. Many people also felt forced to take a Covid vaccine due to social pressure, or because they wanted to have the freedom to travel, work and socialize.

Many people took Covid vaccines enthusiastically in 2021 and have continued to take boosters.

The one-third of people in the US who are unvaccinated have faced discrimination. They have been barred from attending institutes of higher education and barred from many work places which had never required vaccination as a condition of employment before. There were times when they couldn't enter restaurants, bars, gyms or theaters in some states or cross national borders.

The unvaccinated have been dis-invited from weddings, holiday celebrations and other social events once the host knew of their vaccine status. Families and friendship circles, life sustaining relationships, kicked out members who refused to take a Covid vaccine. Some couples divorced when one spouse refused to get a Covid vaccine.

I bet more people have lost friends and family members over the issue of Covid vaccination than they have lost due to SARS-CoV-2.

Most of the people who decided against taking a Covid vaccine had taken all all their childhood vaccinations (Smallpox, Diphtheria, Tetanus, Pertussis, Polio, Measles, Mumps, Rubella, etc) and had vaccinated their children. However, despite that, the unvaccinated were venomously derided as *anti-vaxxers*.

As an unvaccinated person, such anger was shocking to see and experience.

In 2020 and 2021 all Americans were expected to believe in and follow a specific narrative regarding Covid vaccination and Covid mitigation strategies like masking. We were supposed to agree with shutting down schools and closing small independent businesses while Costco and Home Depot stayed open. People who brought up concerns about any part of the Covid narrative were dismissed as conspiracy theorists.

I wrote this book to make the case against Covid vaccine mandates.

I believe that if we lived in a sane and just country truly committed to science there would be no Covid vaccine mandates.

It should be a personal decision whether or not to take a Covid vaccine. We should not be and shouldn't have been mandated to take one.

I hope to prove that point.

# 1... Comparing the number of deaths in 2020 and 2021

*"History, despite its wrenching pain, cannot be unlived, however, if faced with courage, need not be lived again."*

- Maya Angelou (1928-2014) a famous American writer and civil rights activist who wrote biographies, essays, poetry, and plays. She was awarded over 50 honorary degrees.

In this chapter my goal is to show you the rise in deaths involving Covid from 2020 to 2021 (despite vaccination), and the <u>shocking</u> rise in total deaths from any cause in some age groups from 2020 to 2021 Also I include the current Covid vaccination guidelines. My hope is that you question Covid vaccine efficacy and thus the wisdom of Covid vaccine mandates.

I chose to start this book by comparing the number of deaths that occurred in 2020 and 2021. Seeing these numbers at the beginning of the book, will let you know that we are looking at a new situation- one we have never seen before in our lifetimes. The huge increase in the number of deaths is one reason I oppose Covid vaccine mandates. In most age groups there were <u>many more</u> Covid-related deaths and deaths from all causes in 2021 despite widespread vaccination and continuing to follow Covid mitigation strategies like masking, staying home and social distancing in much of the country.

The Covid vaccines aren't working as we had been promised. And something is causing a shocking number of non-Covid related deaths. Things we were told to do did not decrease the number of deaths in 2021. Mass vaccination has not stopped the spread of Covid infections either.

Yet, according to the CDC, mass vaccination and boosters are examples of the tools we have to protect ourselves and others from a Covid infection.

On August 11th 2022, the CDC announced changes to its Covid-19 guidance:

*"Today, CDC is streamlining its COVID-19 guidance to help people better understand their risk, how to protect themselves and others, what actions to take if exposed to COVID-19, and what actions to take if they are sick or test positive for the virus...with more tools— like vaccination, boosters, and treatments....The new Covid policies also include spending less time quarantining when infected: to limit social and economic impacts, quarantine of exposed persons is no longer recommended, regardless of vaccination status."*

The CDC said, "… *spending less time quarantining: to limit social and economic impacts.*"

I wonder if the CDC is finally admitting that there has been a <u>massive amount</u> of financial and psychological damage inflicted upon people in the US due to the Covid mandates that they themselves promoted and most state governments enforced?

I wish the CDC had said that they oppose Covid vaccine mandates. If they had, millions more Americans would finally be able to attend higher education, enter the armed forces and work at a wider variety of jobs. If there had never been vaccine mandates, there would be far less financial and psychological pressure on people today.

In my opinion, the school and business closures and vaccine mandates have done more harm than good.  Did the CDC make these policy changes based on fewer Covid cases and deaths in August 2022, or were their changes politically motivated?

**Cases and Deaths Involving Covid in the US**

Below is a chart showing daily new Covid cases in the US (retrieved from Worldometer August 12, 2022). There were a few stretches of time from March 2020 to April 2022 when there were fewer Covid cases than we saw in August 2022 (indicated by the arrows). Also, note that widespread Covid vaccination in 2021 didn't prevent the massive wave of Covid cases from December 2021 to March 2022. (Vertical lines inserted to show the years.)

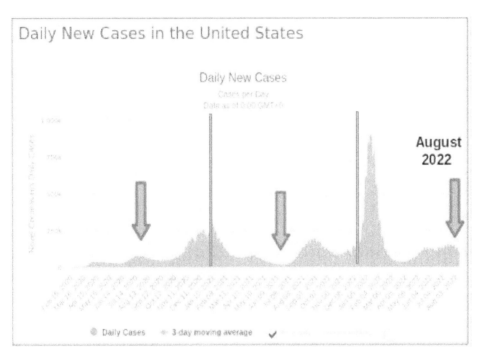

You can see on the Y-axis the number of **Corona virus Daily Cases** are labeled in 250 thousands: 250k, 500k, 750k and 1,000k. We can see that a sizable number of people in the US have had a Covid infection, which offers them some degree of immunity to future Covid infections. Also, we have to add to the number of cases in the chart above the people who had a Covid infection but never took a Covid test. By now, it is highly likely that the vast majority of people in the US have survived a Covid infection.

Let's turn to the number of deaths involving Covid in the US:

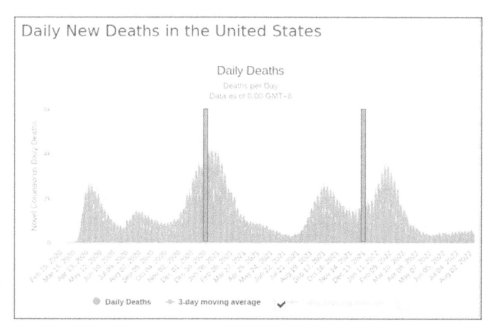

There were five "Covid death waves" in the US between March 2020 and August 2022. Notice the December 2021 to March 2022 death wave that occurred at the same time as the Covid infection wave that we saw in the last chart.

**Did Covid vaccination prevent death?**

Here is a chart showing the daily count of fully vaccinated people from the CDC (retrieved September 11th 2022). The bold line represents the 7- day running average.

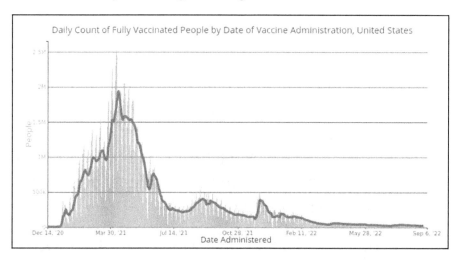

The majority of people were fully vaccinated by the middle of 2021. According to the CDC, by June 24, 2021 vaccinated rates were:

| Age | % Fully Vaccinated |
|---|---|
| **5-11** | 0.4% |
| **12-17** | 26.3% |
| **18-24** | 41.3% |
| **25-49** | 50.4% |
| **50-64** | 66.7% |
| **65 +** | 81% |

The majority of people in the US over the age of 25 were fully vaccinated by June 24th 2021 and over 80% of people over the age of 65, who are most at-risk of death from a Covid infection.

Also, people in many areas in the US were also still masking and social distancing in 2021. We would expect to see fewer Covid-related deaths in 2021, right?

**Here is the CDC table showing deaths involving Covid and deaths from all causes in the US in 2021 by age group:**

| Year | Age Group Years | Deaths involving COVID | Deaths from All Causes |
|---|---|---|---|
| 2021 | 0-17 | 609 | 35789 |
| 2021 | 18-29 | 3933 | 68114 |
| 2021 | 30-39 | 11575 | 104177 |
| 2021 | 40-49 | 26214 | 155548 |
| 2021 | 50-64 | 103176 | 610293 |
| 2021 | 65-74 | 111693 | 725850 |
| 2021 | 75-84 | 110755 | 830710 |
| 2021 | 85 and over | 95251 | 941309 |

**Here is the CDC table showing deaths involving Covid and deaths from all causes in the US in 2020 by age group:**

| Year | Age Group Years | Deaths involving COVID | Deaths from All Causes |
|------|-----------------|------------------------|------------------------|
| 2020 | 0-17 | 199 | 34204 |
| 2020 | 18-29 | 1489 | 63520 |
| 2020 | 30-39 | 4294 | 89319 |
| 2020 | 40-49 | 11336 | 133464 |
| 2020 | 50-64 | 56802 | 557214 |
| 2020 | 65-74 | 82332 | 675940 |
| 2020 | 75-84 | 106319 | 823038 |
| 2020 | 85 and over | 122895 | 1013340 |

**Comparing the number of Deaths from all causes and the number of Deaths involving Covid in 2020 to those in 2021**

I realize we are comparing roughly 9 months of deaths involving Covid in 2020 to 12 months of deaths involving Covid in 2021. However, even if we subtract 25% of the Covid deaths in 2021 to compare roughly 9 months to 9 months, we still see a substantial increase in Covid related deaths in all age groups in 2021 despite vaccination, except for in the 75-84 and 85+ age groups. Recall the percentage of people fully vaccinated by June 24th 2021:

| Age | % Fully Vaccinated |
|-----|--------------------|
| 5-11 | 0.4% |
| 12-17 | 26.3% |
| 18-24 | 41.3% |
| 25-49 | 50.4% |
| 50-64 | 66.7% |
| 65+ | 81% |

Let's compare how many people died in 2020 and 2021, first from all causes (which include Covid) and then deaths involving Covid (numbers below are from the CDC).

## Deaths from all causes and Deaths involving Covid Comparing 2020 and 2021

| Age | Deaths from all causes 2020 | Deaths from all causes 2021 | Deaths involving Covid 2020 | Deaths involving Covid 2021 | Subtracting 25% of 2021 deaths involving Covid |
|---|---|---|---|---|---|
| 0-17 | 34,204 | 35,789 | 199 | 609 | 457 |
| 18-29 | 63,520 | 68,114 | 1,489 | 3,933 | 2,950 |
| 30-39 | 89,319 | **104,177** | 4,294 | 11,575 | 8,681 |
| 40-49 | 133,464 | **155,548** | 11,336 | 26,214 | 19,660 |
| 50-64 | 557,214 | **610,293** | 56,802 | 103,176 | 77,382 |
| 65-74 | 675,940 | 725,850 | 82,332 | 111,693 | 83,770 |
| 75-84 | 823,038 | 830,710 | 106,319 | 110,755 | 83,066 |
| 85+ | 1,013,340 | 941,309 | 122,895 | 95,251 | 71,438 |

**Deaths from all causes**

The number of <u>deaths from all causes</u> increased in 2021 in all age groups except for 85+, which saw a 7.1% decrease. The bolded numbers in the <u>Deaths from all causes 2021</u> column signify a **+9% increase or more.** Why did so many more people die between the ages of 30-64 in 2021?

Let's look specifically at three different age groups to see the percentage of each group's total population who <u>didn't die from any cause</u> in 2020 when there was Covid and no Covid vaccine:

1- I'm in the 50-64 year old age group. There are 62.8 million of us in the US. In 2020, **557,214** people age 50-64 died from something, not necessarily Covid.
That equates to **0.9%** of us dying in 2020 and **99.1%** of us surviving.

2- Let's look at my son's age group. He is part of the 30-39 year old age group. There are 44.7 million people in his age group. In 2020, **89,319** people age 30-39 died from something.
That equates to **0.2%** of people in his age group dying in 2020 and **99.8%** of them surviving.

3- Let's look at children's risk of dying from any cause, age 0-17. There are 71.3 million children in the US. In 2020, **34,204** children died from something.

That equates to **0.048%** children dying from something in 2020 and **99.952%** of them surviving.

**Deaths involving Covid**
The number of deaths involving Covid increased in 2021 from 2020 in all age groups except for the 85+ age group. When comparing 9 months to 9 months, the number of deaths involving Covid still increased in all age groups except for in the 75-84 and 85+ age groups. I seriously doubt the efficacy of Covid vaccines.

In the 50-64 age group there was a dramatic near **82%** increase in deaths involving Covid in 2021. If we adjust the number of deaths in 2021 so that we are comparing roughly 9 months to 9 months, we still see a substantial increase of **36%**. A near **67%** of that population was fully vaccinated before the August-December 2021 wave of Covid infections. What accounted for the huge increase in Covid related deaths when no one in that age group was vaccinated in 2020?

In the 65-74 age group, even when adjusted by 25% and even with an 81% vaccination rate, the number of Covid related deaths in 2021 (83,770) was more than the number in 2020 (82,332). I found that surprising.

All of these increases in death, whether from Covid or from any cause, occurred despite widespread vaccination in 2021 and widespread continuation of Covid mitigation strategies, like masking, school and business closures and social distancing in many states.

Let's look at the chart again more closely to examine the dramatic increase in deaths from all causes and deaths involving Covid in the 30-64 year old age groups to see the percentage increase. I put in the number of deaths related to Covid adjusted for time to compare 9 months to 9 months.

| Age | Deaths from all causes 2020 | Deaths from all causes 2021 | % increase | Deaths involving Covid 2020 | Deaths involving Covid 2021 (adjusted) | % increase |
|---|---|---|---|---|---|---|
| 30-39 | 89,319 | 104,177 | **16.6%** | 4,294 | 8,681 | **102%** |
| 40-49 | 133,464 | 155,548 | **16.5%** | 11,336 | 19,660 | **73%** |
| 50-64 | 557,214 | 610,293 | **9.5%** | 56,802 | 77,382 | **36%** |

It didn't make sense to me that so many more people had a death involving Covid in 2021 when over 50% of the population age 25-64 were fully vaccinated and therefore should have been especially protected them from the wave of deaths August to December 2021. Covid vaccines haven't been working as we had been promised. I imagine many other people were keeping track of the Covid-related deaths in 2020 and 2021 too and were as surprised by these numbers as I was.

**What are the current (September 12ᵗʰ 2022) Covid vaccination guidelines and rates in the US?**

Here are the current CDC Covid vaccination guidelines for people in the US: *"COVID-19 vaccination is recommended for everyone ages 6 months and older in the United States for the prevention of COVID-19. CDC recommends that people get up to date with COVID-19 vaccination. There is currently no FDA-approved or FDA-authorized COVID-19 vaccine for children younger than age 6 months."*

According to the CDC, a total of 67.6% of the entire population is fully vaccinated in the US. 77.4% of the population over the age of 18 is fully vaccinated and 92.1% of the population over the age of 65 are fully vaccinated.

Here are the vaccination rates as of September 12, 2022 according to the CDC data tracker:

| Age | % Fully Vaccinated |
|---------|--------------------|
| Under 2 | 1.1% |
| 2-4 | 2% |
| 5-11 | 31.3% |
| 12-17 | 60.6% |
| 18-24 | 65.1% |
| 25-49 | 70.6% |
| 50-64 | 82.4% |
| 65+ | 92.2% |

Our response to the SARS-CovV-2 virus and the results of mass Covid vaccination will end up in future history books.

In the next chapter we will look at shocking news out of Canada and Washington state.

# 2... Covid deaths in Canada and Washington state in the summer of 2022

*"Investors are sometimes too busy looking for profits to notice where the truth ends and the deception begins."*

Andrew Ross Sorkin (1977-) American journalist and financial columnist for The New York Times.

In this chapter my goal is to show you the number of deaths involving Covid in the vaccinated population vs the unvaccinated people in Canada and in Washington state. My hope is that you will question the wisdom of mandating Covid vaccines.

I live in Ferndale, Washington, close to the Canadian border. I used to go to Canada regularly until the border closed in 2020. When the border reopened in 2021, it was still closed to the unvaccinated.

Despite living much closer to Vancouver BC than to Seattle, I hadn't been able to go to Vancouver until the mandate to be vaccinated to enter Canada ended on October 1st, 2022.

Many people who live in towns near national borders, like Ferndale is to Canada, have relatives in the neighboring country. For example, many people who live in El Paso, Texas have relatives in Mexico and many people who live in southern towns in Switzerland have relatives in Italy. I have unvaccinated friends who have family in Canada who they had not been able to see since March 2020 even though they live only 30 minutes apart.

Moreover, with the closure of the border in 2020, economic activity in my town and in Bellingham (a larger town south of Ferndale) decreased. Here is what Sandy Ward, CEO and President of Bellingham Whatcom County Tourism wrote (July 3rd 2020):

*"The COVID-19 pandemic has had a devastating impact on local jobs. Small businesses, restaurants and lodging have been hit disproportionately hard... information to date suggests a sustained downturn in the economy throughout the summer and into fall* (2020). *Others predict it could be 2021 before a significant recovery starts... in 2019 ...*(tourism and visitors to) *Whatcom County supported **7,443** jobs (in stores, restaurants, attractions, outdoor recreation, lodging, and transportation), with a payroll of **$244.9** million..."*

That's a lot of jobs. What happened to those people? And what happened to the people who sell to those people? Likewise, economic activity in Canada supported by US tourist dollars decreased too.

It was weird for me in 2020 not to see Canadian shoppers at Costco or see the license plates of Canadian drivers on the freeway. I kept thinking about all of the money businesses and families on both sides of the border were losing.

Thankfully, as of October 1st 2022 the Canadian government dropped the mandate to show proof of vaccination at the border. Why did they do that? It may have been because Covid infections and related deaths have decreased and opening the border to the unvaccinated will help boost economic activity, and it could also be because the vaccines haven't been working as we had been promised.

If something really bad was happening in connection to mass Covid vaccination would our governments tell us?

I hate to share this news, but I feel it is necessary because while it is out in the open, it hasn't been investigated and talked about on mainstream media. And it should be public information. We are no less worthy of having a say in matters than the billionaires.  We are impacted by their dictates because billionaires essentially control our government and our media. We only get to hear what they want us to hear.

**From June 14th- August 28th 2022 at least 86% of deaths involving Covid In Canada were among the vaccinated (boosted included).** The following chart is taken from the Canadian government's  September 23, 2022 update, and shows the number of cases, hospitalizations and deaths by vaccination status in Canada through **August 28th 2022**:

Outcomes of confirmed COVID-19 cases reported to PHAC by vaccination status, as of August 28, 2022

| Status | Cases | Hospitalizations | Deaths |
|---|---|---|---|
| Unvaccinated | 993,242 | 55,040 | 10,673 |
| Primary series completed | 787,721 | 22,601 | 3,730 |
| Primary series completed and 1 additional dose | 442,357 | 23,909 | 4,830 |
| Primary series completed and 2 or more additional doses | 37,924 | 2,444 | 780 |

Here are what the death numbers look like as a chart:

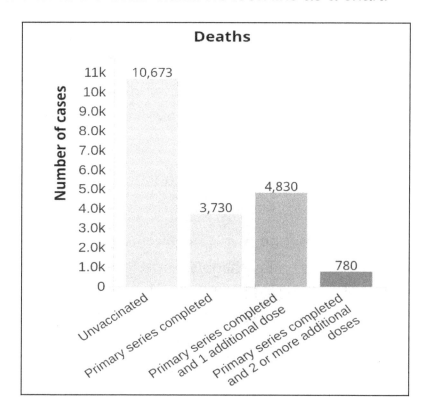

Unfortunately, the numbers given are a little deception because they are providing a cumulative (running total) of deaths that stretches all the way back to the start of Covid in 2020 – before Covid vaccines were even introduced. Thankfully, the Canadian government archives its earlier reports. Therefore, we can easily compare the September 23rd report to earlier reports, and by doing subtraction we can then figure out the number of deaths that occurred in a given time period and the vaccine status of the people who died.

The following table was taken from a Canadian government report published on July 1st 2022, and it shows the cumulative number of cases, hospitalizations and deaths by vaccination status through June 12th 2022.

| Characteristics and severe outcomes associated unvaccinated, partially vaccinated and fully vaccinated confirmed cases reported to PHAC, as of June 12, 2022 | | | |
| --- | --- | --- | --- |
| **Status** | **Cases** | **Hospitalizations** | **Deaths** |
| Unvaccinated | 969,484 | 53,177 | 10,369 |
| Fully vaccinated | 780,941 | 20,693 | 3,550 |
| Fully vaccinated with 1 additional dose | 353,930 | 17,653 | 3,707 |
| Fully vaccinated with 2 or more additional doses | 13,157 | 694 | 242 |

Here are what the death numbers look like as a chart:

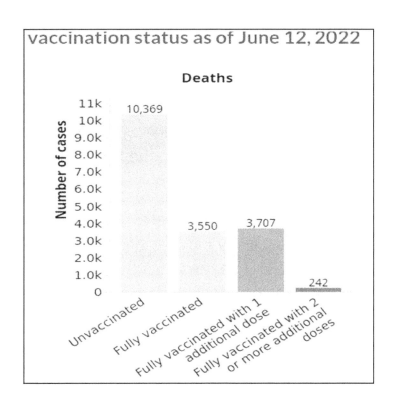

Here is a table showing how to subtract the cumulative deaths on June 12$^{th}$ from the cumulative deaths on August 28$^{th}$:

| Date | Unvaxxed (and partially vaxxed) | Fully Vaxxed (2 shots plus 2 weeks) | Fully Vaxxed plus 1 booster | Fully Vaxxed plus 2 or more boosters |
|---|---|---|---|---|
| August 28 | 10673 | 3730 | 4830 | 780 |
| June 12 | 10369 | 3550 | 3707 | 242 |
| **Difference** | **304** | **180** | **1123** | **538** |

By doing simple subtraction we see that that between June 12th and August 28th 2022, **1,841 fully vaccinated (boosted included) people died** while 304 unvaccinated people died. **The total number of deaths involving Covid were 2,145 and of those, 1,841 were fully vaccinated (including boosted) which is 86%.**

(According to Our World in Data, approximately 83% of Canada's population is fully vaccinated.)

It's pretty surprising how the vaccines aren't working as promised, but the mainstream media isn't talking about it and the mandates in the US are continuing. If the vaccines aren't working in Canada, I can assure you they aren't working here in the US either.

However, even that startling 86% of deaths in the vaccinated group doesn't tell the complete truth. The reason is that the deaths in the unvaccinated group most likely include the deaths of people who were partially vaccinated.  The reason is that a person is not considered "fully vaccinated" until 14 days after getting their second shot. For example, a person could get a Covid vaccine on November 2nd, and then get a Covid infection and die on November 14th, and he or should would be counted as unvaccinated. The Canadian government didn't make a column for the number of partially vaccinated people who died. Instead, they put partially vaccinated people in the unvaccinated category.

This news that 86% of deaths related to Covid occurred in the fully vaccinated (including the boosted) between June 12th and August 28th 2022 would shock the public. Why aren't Canadians being made aware of this via their media? The numbers are readily available, yet it seems no journalist is keeping track of them. I thought journalism was supposed to be  important to a functioning Democracy.

I live in Washington state. On the Washington State Dept of Health website there is a report called **SARS-CoV-2 Vaccine Breakthrough Surveillance and Case Information Resource**. In this report the Washington State Department of Health tells us the number of fully vaccinated people who got a Covid infection and the number of fully vaccinated people who died. (Fully vaccinated people also include people who were boosted.) The report is updated monthly.

Here is an image from the January 17, 2021 to July 30, 2022 report:

**COVID-19 deaths among SARS-CoV-2 breakthrough cases in Washington State**

January 17, 2021 - July 30, 2022

Among breakthrough cases from this surveillance period **2,979** have died of COVID-related illness.

The age range of deceased cases was 15 - 106 years (median 79 years).

From January 17 2021 – July 30 2022 there were **2,979** Covid-related deaths in fully vaccinated people. Here is an image from the January 17 2021 - September 24 2022 report:

**COVID-19 deaths among SARS-CoV-2 breakthrough cases in Washington State**

January 17, 2021 - September 24, 2022

Among breakthrough cases from this surveillance period **3,373** have died of COVID-related illness.

The age range of deceased cases was 15 - 106 years (median 79 years).

Among the **3,373** deceased:

From January 17th 2021– September 24th 2022 there were **3,373** Covid-related deaths in fully vaccinated people.

Subtracting the total number of breakthrough Covid-related deaths as of July 30th from the number of breakthrough Covid-related deaths as of September 24th, we can ascertain that between July 30th and September 24th there were a total of **394** Covid-related deaths in the fully vaccinated.

From the Washington State Dept of health, there is a chart that shows the cumulative total of people who have had Covid-related deaths where you can find the total number of Covid-related deaths between two time periods:

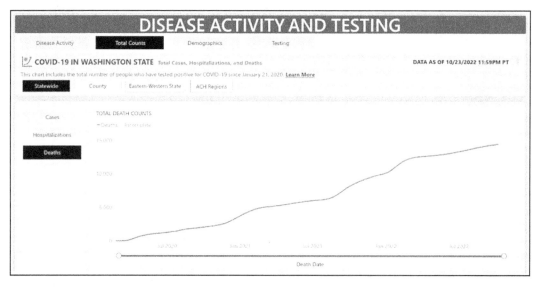

Using the scroll bar on the trendline, **13,730** people had had a Covid-related death by July 30th and by September 24th there were a total of **14,366** deaths. Subtracting the two numbers we find that a total of **636** people died with/ from Covid in the July 30th-September 24th time frame. Out of those 636 deaths involving Covid, **394** occurred in fully vaccinated people, meaning that **62% of Covid deaths from July 30th to September 24th 2022 occurred in the vaccinated.**

Covid vaccines- Not as effective as we had been promised, right?

I think we have been terribly misled.

And we also knew about the risks associated with Covid vaccination early in 2021. Here is a Canadian actress named named Jennifer Gibson who told her story in a May 27th 2021 video, in which she openly shares:

*"So I got it [Bell's Palsy]* **about two weeks after getting my vaccine**, *and I had a* **rough go** *with the vaccine — and I* **guess still am**.*"*

and adds*: "But I have to say that I* **would do it again** *because it's what we have to do to see people."*

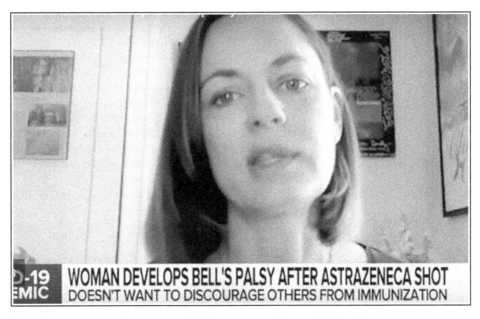

WOMAN DEVELOPS BELL'S PALSY AFTER ASTRAZENECA SHOT
DOESN'T WANT TO DISCOURAGE OTHERS FROM IMMUNIZATION

What has happened to people's reasoning ability?

I want the people responsible for developing Covid vaccine mandate policies and the people who are enforcing them and supporting them to be aware of what has been going on with the Covid vaccines - and be held to account.

They need to publicly apologize for what they have done to us. They might need to be imprisoned.

In the next chapter we will look at the shared experience we had in 2020. We really have been through some extremely unusual times.

# 3... Our Shared Experience

*A people without the knowledge of their past history, origin and culture is like a tree without roots.*

-Marcus Garvey (1887-1940) was a political activist, publisher, journalist, entrepreneur, and orator, who was born in Jamaica and moved to the US at the age of 39. He established the Negro Factories Corporation as well as a chain of restaurants and grocery stores, laundries, a hotel, and a printing press. He taught the importance of having economic strength.

In this chapter my goal is to share with the experiences that most of us shared and can relate to that occurred in 2020. I hope that you will consider writing down your memories and give them to a younger person. We lived through history.

Most all of us recall the following events in 2020:

On January 12th the World Health Organization reported the first Covid related death in Wuhan, China.

On February 5th 2020 the Gates Foundation donated $79 million to Imperial College in London, which recommended Covid mitigation strategies to governments and public health agencies around the world. The US response to Covid was in line with Imperial College's recommendations.

The first Covid death in the US was reportedly on February 6th. (however, it has been reported that a few people may have died in January 2020.)

On February 28th 2020, the virus was detected at *Life Care Center of Kirkland*, a nursing home near Seattle, Washington. Reportedly 57% of the residents there were hospitalized and of those 25% died.

On March 16, 2020, President Trump issued an order to shut down the country for 15 days to slow the spread of Covid, to "flatten the curve."

We were told to stay at home, and if we had to go out, to maintain a six foot distance from other people. 15 days at home to flatten the curve turned into a lot longer depending on the state a person was in. In Washington state, the stay at home orders were lifted on May 31st 2020, over two months later, and in New Mexico they weren't lifted until August 28th 2020.

**Leaving the workplace behind**
Many Americas had to leave their workplaces in 2020. We had that shared experience. Office buildings, small businesses and schools shut down. Millions of people began working online from home and millions of children began studying online from home. We also learned in 2020 that some workers were essential, like grocery store clerks and medical workers and could continue going to their workplaces while other workers were non-essential. Restaurant workers were deemed non-essential.

Because of having to lockdown, many small businesses closed their doors permanently. Yelp, which is an online directory for local businesses, reported on the number of businesses that had permanently closed by August 31st 2020 in their **September 2020 Yelp: Local Economy Impact Report** (my bolding):

"As of August 31, **163,735 total US. businesses on Yelp have closed** since the beginning of the pandemic (observed as March 1), a 23% increase since July 10. In the wake of COVID-19 cases increasing and local restrictions continuing to change in many states we're seeing both permanent and temporary closures rise across the nation, with **60% of those closed businesses not reopening (97,966 permanently closed)."**

Nearly 98,000 businesses advertised on Yelp shut down permanently. That's in addition to the however many businesses shut down permanently that are not on Yelp. I wonder how many people were financially impoverished due to the decision to lockdown. I wonder in the future if most people will look back at 2020 and wish we hadn't shut down "non-essential" businesses.

Let's hear from some black owned business owners whose businesses were shut down permanently:

In the Burlington County Times article **South Jersey Black small business owners don't sugarcoat negative impacts of COVID** (August 15, 2022) we read (my underlining):

"*According to data from the consulting firm McKinsey & Company, 41% of Black-owned businesses (in the US) were lost during the first few months of the pandemic, accounting for the largest loss across racial demographics.*

*Jermaine Hatcher, owner of J&J Janitorial Cleaning Services in Camden, shared his challenge is with many economic relief programs designed for small businesses. As micro-business owner, he said he is often forgotten about or has a more difficult time obtaining money due to not having enough employees to be recognized as a small business.*

*"To be considered a small business, you have to have 10 full-time employees," Hatcher said. "A lot of us want to scale up where as though we can have employees that we can give benefits to and give a living wage to so it's like how do we scale up from being micro to small?"*

*Tony Williams, owner of Seafood Haven in Willingboro, shared a similar experience while trying to get funding for his business "I think one of the barriers I faced was that I didn't have any employees. I'm an educator so I hire my students, family members, and because of the fact that I didn't have employees that I had a 1099 for or paid income wage taxes oftentimes that put me at the bottom of the pile," Williams said. "Finally when I was approved, I was told there was no more money and that was so frustrating."*

I was at a community college teaching English (to speakers of other languages-ESL) at the time of the lockdown in March 2020. The college's executive team told the teachers that we would have to leave campus and teach our courses online for the 2-3 weeks remaining in the quarter.

I had a feeling at the time that teaching online would continue for much longer.

Teachers were able to meet their students one last time face to face in class before starting to teach online from home. Most of my students were from mainland China. Two of them were from Wuhan and one of them knew someone who had died from Covid in Wuhan. All of my students were extremely nervous about the Covid-19 virus and were very worried that I might die (I was 58 years old at the time). Before coming to class on our last day to meet face to face, the students gathered together the N-95 masks they felt they could spare and gave me ten. I graciously accepted the masks.

I took my ten N-95 masks to a department meeting right after class that day. All of the teachers at the meeting were feeling heightened by the news of the pandemic and having to finish the quarter online. I asked if anyone wanted one of the N-95 masks. No one wanted a mask.

And then masks became like gold. Do you remember the mask shortage?

Teaching online from home for a few weeks turned into a year and a half.

**The effects of the shutdowns on children**
In addition to business shutdowns, which led to poverty, depression and many other problems, at parks near my house, I saw orange tape surrounding the play equipment, a warning to all of the danger that the corona virus virus might be on the play equipment.

Many millions of children nationwide were deprived of exercise, playing in groups and seeing faces, which are very important parts of child development. When they did return to school, over a year later, most children had to wear masks, which was contrary to numerous studies. It was evident when they returned to school that many children suffered from severe mental health issues and a massive loss of learning. Reports from teachers show that their classroom behavior had changed as well.

We have allowed children to be damaged, perhaps beyond repair, and in my opinion unnecessarily. Meanwhile the crafters of Covid talking points told us "Children are resilient." Are they?

According to the article **Cambridge Study: Children's Mental Health Deteriorated 'Substantially' During Lockdown** (December 11, 2020): *"Keeping children away from sandboxes and swing sets, or depriving them of small birthday parties and playdates, is doing more harm than good—particularly where children are mostly spared from the worst effects of COVID-19 and their risk of dying from COVID-19 is, thankfully, extremely low. By contrast, the harm of lockdowns and other pandemic policies and practices that deprive young people of social connection is disturbingly high..."*

**We all have Covid stories.**
Another similarity nearly all of us share is that we have stories about Covid infections and death, wearing masks, socially distancing, taking careful walks, working from home, feeling afraid, etc. I think you should write down your Covid stories to pass along to the younger generation. We are living through history.

I know of an unvaccinated young man in his early 20's who had a Covid infection and went to the hospital because he couldn't breathe, and he died. His family claims he died because of the medical treatment he was given and they took legal action.

I know of an elderly woman in her 80's, the mother of one of my husband's students, who, while in a hospital actively dying of cancer, tested positive for Covid. And when she died of cancer soon after being admitted, her death was labeled Covid. Her family complained.

I know of an apparently healthy 40 year old vaccinated woman who died in her sleep.

One of my previous coworkers has a vaccine injury and has a hard time working. I know several vaccine injured people on social media.

And for all lives lost to Covid I'm truly sad.

**We most all agree that there is a Corona virus**

I have a great degree of respect for SARS-Cov-2. It sounds weird to have respect for a virus. Like most people in the US, since March 2020, I have taken special care of my health and have tried to protect myself from Covid-19. I avoid crowded places, and I am happy because it seems like sick people are staying home more than they were before 2020. I can't remember the last time I saw a person cough, sneeze or blow their nose in public.

Right when I found out most people who die from a Covid infection are obese, I lost 20 pounds and strive to maintain a normal weight.

Still today in late 2022, I disinfect my counters, bathrooms and tables nearly every day and wash my hands a lot. I take vitamins C, D3 and a multivitamin most everyday and sometimes zinc and Quercetin if I am going to be in a crowd. I spend 3-5 hours outside most days and I avoid crowds and indoor spaces with low ventilation. I kept my windows open as much as possible in 2020 and 2021.

Aside from disagreeing on the issues of small business and school closures and masking, most Americans were united in their attempts to protect themselves and others from Covid in 2020.

One important thing that very few of us knew about in 2020 was the 2017 meeting that Bill Gates, billionaire and person of influence, had with President Trump. President Trump shared with Gates that he was considering starting a commission to look into the ill effects of vaccines. Bill Gates can be seen in a video talking about his response to Trump's idea. He said (my bolding):

*"... A guy named Robert F. Kennedy was advising him (Trump) that vaccines were causing bad things and I said '**No, that's a dead end. That would be a bad thing. Don't do that.**"*

You should see Gates' body language in the video.

Why would Gates be against the US having a vaccine safety and efficacy committee? The video is so weird!

You can see the video on the Jimmy Dore YouTube channel in the September 18th show **Bill Gates Stopped Trump From Investigating Vaccines.** Jimmy Dore is a comedian turned news commentator. The video is well worth watching.

It doesn't seem like we are allowed to have an independent and impartial (not related to big pharma or to the elite, like Bill Gates) group of scientists in the US analyzing both the Covid vaccines' effectiveness and its safety. There has been a lot of things going on behind the scenes which led to the vaccine mandates in 2021 and to the CDC adding the Covid vaccine to the Children's vaccine schedule in October 2022.

In the next chapter we look at some of the things many Americans were learning that made them decide against taking a Covid vaccine in 2021.

# 4... The Road Less Traveled

The Road Not Taken

*Two roads diverged in a yellow wood,*
*And sorry I could not travel both*
*And be one traveler, long I stood*
*And looked down one as far as I could*
*To where it bent in the undergrowth;*

*Then took the other, as just as fair,*
*And having perhaps the better claim,*
*Because it was grassy and wanted wear...*

*I shall be telling this with a sigh*
*Somewhere ages and ages hence:*
*Two roads diverged in a wood, and I—*
*I took the one less traveled by,*
*And that has made all the difference.*

-Robert Frost (1874-1963) was a beloved American poet who used a rural background to explore complex social and philosophical themes. He was the only poet to receive 4 Pulitzer prizes for poetry.

In this chapter my goal is to share with you the information many unvaccinated people were learning in 2020 and 2021 which led them to decide against taking a Covid vaccine. I hope you will appreciate how many people were doing research.

**Sweden**

Sweden's response to Covid in 2020 was one of my first experiences disagreeing with the seeming majority of Americans (or at least my friends and acquaintances) on anything related to Covid.

I was a supporter of Sweden's approach to Covid which differed from the US's approach. Sweden never had stay at home orders and their businesses remained open (thus, a distinction wasn't made between essential and non-essential businesses and workers). Sweden didn't shut down its elementary schools or force children to be masked, and Swedish children could play in parks. Their kids could be kids and they didn't die and weren't seen as Covid vectors.

And while some high schools and colleges did close, it was for a short time. Also, Swedes didn't seem to socially distance, wear masks or be afraid. The Swedish people basically lived normally, and as a result, they haven't suffered economically or psychologically nearly as much as people have in the US.

The mistake that Sweden did make is that many Covid patients were put into nursing homes. Nearly half of Sweden's Covid-related deaths had occurred in nursing homes by November 2020.

We all saw Sweden heavily demonized and ridiculed in the US in 2020. How is Sweden doing now compared to the US? According to **Real Clear Politics**, which has an up to date Corona virus tracker: (Corona virus (COVID-19) Global Deaths), the August 11, 2022 Covid death rate per million was: **US: 3,243 and Sweden: 1,910.** The infection fatality rate is: US: 1.12% and Sweden: 0.76%

The infection fatality rate (IFR) is the percentage used to show the percentage of people with a Covid infection who die. In the US just over 1% of people who have a Covid infection die while in Sweden 0.76% of people with a Covid infection die.

Here is a comparison of the cumulative deaths (a running record of the total deaths) from **Our World in Data**. You can see that Sweden had more deaths per million than the US for a short while in early 2020. Since that time, Sweden has had far fewer deaths despite not locking down or masking.

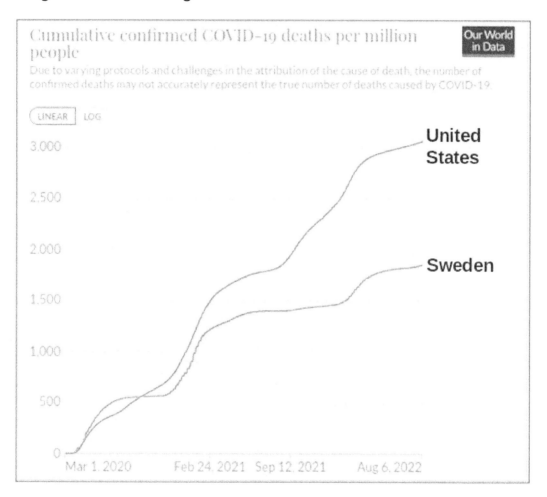

I didn't understand the demonization against Sweden in 2020. How was it possible to know in 2020 how Sweden would fare in the long run when we didn't know much about Covid-19 at the time? I was watching a battle of belief systems - people arguing about an unknown future. Seeing the knee-jerk demonization of Sweden made me realize our news was being influenced by one-sided forces like billionaires.

Below is another chart from **Our World in Data** comparing the percentage of excess mortality (deaths) between the US and Sweden. Excess mortality means more people died in a year than were expected that year, usually determined by the previous 4-5 year average number of deaths:

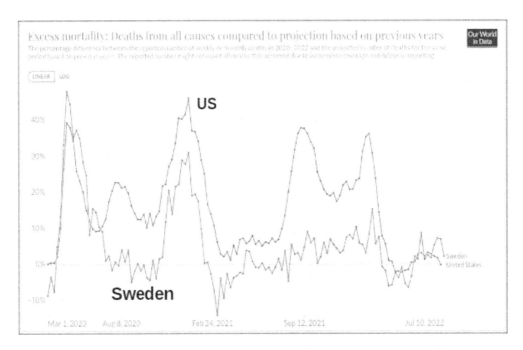

In the chart above, the Y-axis shows us the percentage of excess death from all causes (not just Covid). The percentage of excess deaths in Sweden was greater than the percentage of excess deaths in the US for several weeks at the beginning of the pandemic until roughly mid-June 2020. Since three months into the pandemic, the percentage of excess deaths in Sweden had been consistently much lower than the percentage of excess deaths in the US. Only from roughly July 2022 was the percentage of excess deaths slightly greater in Sweden. The sheer number of excess deaths from all causes (not just Covid) in the US is pretty shocking, By the end of September 2020 Sweden had suffered 5,900 deaths related to Covid, more per 100,000 than its Nordic neighbors but fewer than countries like Spain and Italy which had opted for hard lockdowns.

Fast forward to vaccines: Sweden doesn't recommend giving Covid vaccines to children under 12, and people under the age of 30 years aren't given the Moderna vaccine due to the risk of inflammation of the heart (myocarditis) and risk of inflammation of the sack that holds the heart (pericarditis).

**Independent Media**

A person's decision whether or not to get a Covid vaccine largely depended on where they got their information. If they were getting their news from media sources, like CNN, MSNBC, and the New York Times as well as from government public health agencies and elected leaders, they tended to view Covid vaccination favorably. If they were getting their information from independent sources, like the many doctors and scientists who questioned Covid vaccination, they viewed Covid vaccines with skepticism. Unvaccinated people have tended to read more independent media than vaccinated people it seems.

Many unvaccinated people already had a healthy distrust of mainstream media, big pharma and government leaders well before Covid, so they didn't exactly rush out to get a Covid vaccine when they were encouraged to get one. It's not like we have never been lied to or propagandized as a people, right?

Also, the very act of barring the many doctors and scientists who questioned Covid vaccination from speaking in mainstream media was suspicious. Why were some highly credentialed voices allowed to be heard in 2020 and 2021 while others were dismissed and ridiculed?

In independent media we learned about the many doctors, nurses, and scientists in the US who chose not to take a Covid vaccine and subsequently lost their jobs. Isn't it in the public interest to know why highly credentialed medical workers refused Covid vaccination?

After the vaccines campaign started in 2021, it was broadcast widely in mainstream media that a huge segment of our population was "vaccine-hesitant". And worse than that, there was also free flowing demonization of the unvaccinated on TV talk shows, in social media and in normal conversation. In my opinion, that such demonization was acceptable to anyone in the US served as a barometer of our nation's mental health.  Some Americans seeing this prejudice and discrimination being aimed at them became obsessed with learning all they could about Covid vaccines and the closure and mask mandates. And as a result, they lost even more trust in mainstream media, public health, hospitals and the government. What did they learn exactly?

**The Covid Death Profile**
Many people learned about the Covid-19 death profile in 2020, the age and underlying health of people who were dying from a Covid-19 infection. And ascertaining their own personal risk, they decided against taking a Covid vaccine.

Incidentally, did you know that the CDC refers to Covid deaths as "Deaths <u>involving</u> Covid"? The word "involving" doesn't exactly mean "cause". Money played a role in writing *Covid* on hospital admission forms and on death certificates as well. Hospitals got paid extra for caring for Covid patients who lived or died. The CARES act gave hospitals an extra 20% reimbursement for medicare patients, and the federal government gave hospitals in high risk areas extra money too. According to a July 30th 2020 ABC 10 news report out of Sacramento California (my underlining):

*"… earlier this month, Health and Human Services announced a second round of federal relief for hospitals in high impact areas totaling $10 billion. … HHS reported 63 California hospitals received <u>$50,000 for each eligible corona virus patient they admitted between Jan. 1 and June 10, 2020</u>.... a combined total of $607 million."*

## How many people died who weren't vaccinated?

The table below shows the number of Covid related deaths in different age groups in 2020 (numbers from the CDC). You will see the approximate population of each age group, followed by the number of deaths from any cause, followed by the number of deaths involving Covid. Finally, you will see the percentage of deaths that involved Covid out of the total number of deaths from any cause for each age group.

I put in a thick line to show the stark difference between younger and older populations. The thick line helps us see how much less risk people under the age of 40 have of dying from anything, let alone Covid, than people in the 3 oldest age groups.

**US: Deaths from all causes and Covid related deaths-2020**

| Age | Approximate population | Total deaths from all causes | Total number of Deaths involving Covid | % of deaths involving Covid out of total deaths |
|---|---|---|---|---|
| 0-17 | 71.3 million | 34204 | 199 | 0.6% |
| 18-29 | 48.8 million | 63520 | 1489 | 2.3% |
| 30-39 | 44.7 million | 89319 | 4294 | 4.8% |
| 40-49 | 40.3 million | 133,464 | 11,336 | 8.5% |
| 50-64 | 62.8 million | 557,214 | 56,802 | 10.2% |
| 65-74 | 32.5 million | 675,940 | 82,332 | 12.2% |
| 75-84 | 16.5 million | 823,038 | 106,319 | 12.9% |
| 85+ | 6.7 million | 1,013,340 | 122,895 | 12.1% |

In all of 2020, according to the CDC, there were fewer than 6,000 Covid related deaths in the entire US among the 165 million people under the age of 40. There was no vaccine and very few young people died when taking into account their entire population.

We can also see patterns in this chart. For one, the older a person is the greater chance he or she has of dying from any cause. Compare 34,204 deaths from any cause in the 0-17 year old group, which has a population of over 70 million to the over 1 million deaths from any cause in the 85+ group, which has a population of only 6.7 million.

Also, the number of deaths involving Covid increases dramatically as a person ages. Compare **1,489** deaths involving Covid in the 18-29 year old age group, which has a population of nearly 49 million to the **106,319** deaths involving Covid in the 75-84 year old age group, which has a much smaller population of 16.5 million.

The chance of a person under the age of 30 dying from a Covid infection is very very small. **There is a 2,100 x greater chance that a 75 year old dies from Covid-related causes than a 20 year old.**

Now, let's turn to the percentages. Note the percentage of Covid-related deaths out of deaths from all causes in each age group. For example, in 2020 in the 0-17 age group, Covid-related deaths accounted for a mere 0.6% of that group's total number of deaths. 99.4% of the children who died died from other causes. In the 85+ group Covid-related deaths comprised 12.1% of their total deaths. 87.9% of people over the age of 85 died from something else.

I am 61 years old. If I were to die, there would be a near 90% chance that it would be from something other than Covid-19.

Finally, we can see that in 2020 over 80% of deaths involving Covid occurred in people over the age of 65 with over 60% occurring in people over the age of 75. Just over 1.5% of deaths involving Covid occurred in people under the age of 40. Young adults age 18-29 make up 0.4% of all Covid deaths. Here is how the proportion of deaths involving Covid by age looks in a pie chart:

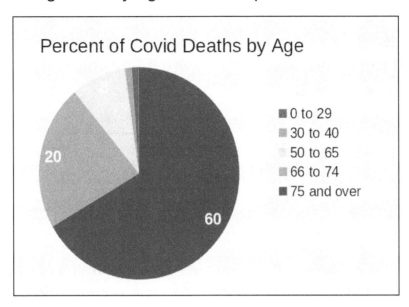

The mainstream media neglected to talk much about how a Covid infection is WAY more life threatening to people the older they are and the weaker their immune system is. Instead, the mainstream media pushed an especially fearful narrative as if everyone had an equal chance of dying from Covid. As a result of fear-mongering, in 2021 many workplaces, the armed forces and college and university campuses mandated the uptake of a risky vaccine despite the fact that virtually no healthy person of a healthy weight under the age of 40 dies from Covid.

I never saw anyone on mainstream media talk about how people under the age of 40 virtually always recover from a Covid infection, not to mention how older people typically survive a Covid infection too. Why did so many people in the US dutifully do what they were told when the truth was that not much was known about the safety or efficacy of Covid vaccines? Remember these vaccines got emergency use authorization. In 2022, they are still experimental.

## Comorbidities

In addition to seeing the age distribution of people who had a death involving Covid in 2020, we learned that nearly everyone who had a death involving Covid had 2+ comorbidities, which means underlying health problems, like lung disease, diabetes, high blood pressure, obesity and kidney disease. There were many articles like this one in Time magazine (April 22, 2020):

> Almost Every Hospitalized Coronavirus Patient
> Has Another Underlying Health Issue,
> According to a Study of New York Patients

In this article we learned that nearly every person in a NY hospital admitted for a Covid infection had one or more comorbidities:
Hypertension- 53.1%
Obesity (BMI ≥30) – 41.7%
Diabetes – 31.7%
Morbid Obesity (BMI ≥35) – 19%
Coronary artery disease- 10.4%
Asthma – 8.4%
Congestive heart failure – 6.5%
(The article went on to list more comorbidities.)

In 2020 we also learned that the average age of a Covid-related death was 76, nearly 80% of people who died were obese, most had low levels of vitamin D and approximately 40% of Covid-related deaths occurred in nursing homes.

I became especially suspicious of the Covid-related messaging in 2020 and 2021 when I didn't hear about vitamin D or obesity in the news. (Though the following article is from 2022, information about vitamin D was easy to find in 2020 and 2021.)

An article out of UC Davis Health entitled **What is the link between vitamin D levels and COVID-19?** (February 15, 2022) explains a study on vitamin D conducted in Israel (my underlining):

*"(The study) found that people with a vitamin D deficiency are more likely to develop a severe or critical case of COVID-19 compared to people who had sufficient levels of the vitamin in their blood.*

*Patients with a vitamin D deficiency were* **14 times** *more likely to have a severe or critical case of COVID-19. Additionally,* <u>the mortality rate for those with insufficient vitamin D levels was 25.6%, compared with 2.3% among those with adequate levels."</u>

I wonder if any lives would have been saved if we, as a nation, had gone on a health kick to lose weight and taken low-cost Vitamin D?

Some articles in 2021, discredited the notion that low vitamin D levels contributed to the deaths in people with severe Covid. Also, absent from media was the concept of natural immunity, which means your immune system knows how to successfully fight off an infection because of having survived an earlier infection. It was as if natural immunity had never existed before in history. I noted its absence in everything I was seeing on TV and in media and it didn't make sense.

Thankfully, in 2022 the CDC acknowledged natural immunity in their August 11 2022 updated Covid guidelines. They stated there is a high level of immunity in the population from "both the vaccines and infections" so the virus now poses a much lower risk to public health.

Many Americans have refused a Covid vaccine because they are healthy and have no underlying health conditions and they were paying attention to who was dying. And personally, in 2021, after I had learned about the vaccine injuries that were occurring, I couldn't understand why any healthy person of a normal weight with no comorbidities would take one.

## Vaccine Injuries

In 2021 many people learned about Covid vaccine injuries. Serious injuries, like permanent paralysis, myocarditis, miscarriage and even death, were occurring shortly after vaccination in otherwise healthy people, especially after the second dose or a booster. One source of information has been the VAERS data base, which is a vaccine injury reporting agency co-managed by the FDA and the CDC. According to studies, vaccine injuries are under-reported to VAERS.

Here is a summary of some of the injuries (and deaths) associated with Covid vaccines from January 2021 – August 16th 2022 in the US:

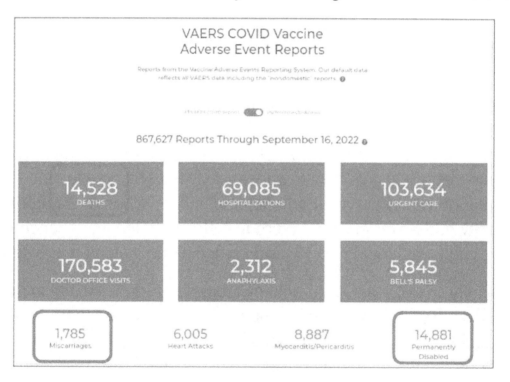

Is it reasonable to mandate a vaccine that has been associated with over 14,500 deaths, 1,785 miscarriages and well over 14,800 permanent disabilities?

Is it ethical to mandate that people take risks with their health?

Can you imagine being a healthy person in your 20's who takes a Covid vaccine and ends up permanently disabled? Mandating Covid vaccination is not the same as mandating seat belts. The seat belt mandate analogy doesn't work because the act of wearing a seat belt isn't associated with your death or permanent disability. And evidence clearly shows that Covid vaccines are not saving lives.

Here is a vaccine injured person named Michelle. She asks the many people who dismiss vaccine injuries and claim VAERS isn't reliable where the vaccine injured people should go to be counted:

Michelle @michellespj · 13h

When people here say "vax injures are rare", what source are you using for that statement? The gov't? They haven't counted me. They claim VAERS isn't a reliable source, so where should I, and all other vaccine injured people, go to get counted? Tell us. We deserve to be counted!

○ 72    ↩ 464    ♥ 1,573    ↑

Many doctors in the US and worldwide are paying attention to injuries associated with Covid vaccines. Cardiologist Anish Koka MD published an article on Substack entitled **Vaccine myocarditis update from Thailand** (August 10th 2022). In it he describes how 3 out of 301 Thai children age 13-18 who took a Covid vaccine ended up hospitalized with myocarditis. He concludes his article by saying (my underlining):

*"...administration of a therapeutic (Covid vaccine) requires an understanding of the risks of the therapy being offered. <u>The US has done an unbelievably poor job of defining that risk to the population since myocarditis was first reported as an adverse event related to the vaccines in April of 2021.</u> The Thai study helps fill in some of the data void so parents and their doctors can be better informed when discussing the risks and benefits of the vaccines."*

Down the other path of trusting Anthony Fauci, the CDC and mainstream media, there has been little to no talk about vaccine injuries, which are also known as "adverse events". It was as if they haven't been occurring. In my opinion, too many Americans have either supported or haven't questioned Covid vaccine mandates.

By the summer of 2021 it has felt like we are living in two different worlds.

**Who are the unvaccinated?**
Trying to capture the unvaccinated as a demographic is impossible. We are from every race, religion (or not religious), every political party, every age group, and every income level. The old and the young, highly educated or not, rich or poor- we are probably the most diverse group of people in the US.

The media started calling us "vaccine hesitant" early on in 2021. However, it has been my experience that people who chose not to get a Covid vaccine were not vaccine hesitant. That label implies we were scared of shots, like children are scared of shots. The word hesitant gives the impression that we could be soothed into taking the vaccine or talked into taking it. In my opinion, the term *vaccine hesitancy* was a slick Madison Avenue marketing ploy. **We weren't hesitant. We had made an informed decision for ourselves.**

The questions we have about Covid vaccines include:


1- Covid vaccines come with risks. Is it OK to mandate that people take risks with their health?

2- Why mandate a vaccine to enter higher education when very few college age people have deaths involving Covid and the Covid vaccine doesn't prevent infection, transmission or death?

3-Why haven't dissenting doctors and scientists been given space in newspapers and in mainstream media? Why have they been so readily dismissed by fact checkers and subjected to cancel culture?

4- Why hasn't the mainstream media and public health been telling us about the Covid vaccine injuries that have been occurring?

5- Why are Covid vaccines being pushed on babies and children?

6- Why haven't we been given updates on how Covid vaccines are preventing death in people under the age of 74? How about a story talking about how high levels of Covid vaccination coupled with surviving infections brought us to herd immunity? The media can't give us these updates or stories because neither preventing death or herd immunity is something they can report on.

In the next chapter we look at nine specific reasons why one-third of people in the US refused to take a Covid vaccine in 2021.

# 5... Nine reasons people chose not to get a Covid vaccine

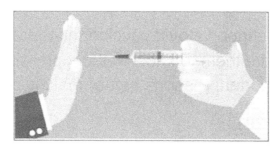

*"Illinois health care workers who were fired or otherwise impacted by their hospitals' Covid-19 vaccine mandate will receive a $10 million settlement after filing a lawsuit challenging the rule... The settlement approved in the Illinois Northern District Court will result in 473 employees of the system becoming eligible for compensation for being denied a religious exemption to the vaccine mandate..."*
Fox Business, August 15th 2022

In this chapter my goal is to share share some of the reasons that unvaccinated people chose not to take a Covid vaccine. I hope you will see that it was a reasonable decision to make and yet people lost their jobs and young people weren't allowed to attend college.

If a person doesn't want to take a Covid vaccine, he or she shouldn't lose their job. It's immoral and capricious to mandate Covid vaccination in order to work. A big thank you to the Illinois healthcare workers who spoke out and to the judge in Illinois who ruled in their favor! Like most unvaccinated people, I believe that the Corona virus is real and has contributed to the deaths of many people. The CDC reports that Covid infections have contributed to the deaths of well over 1 million people in the US, yet I decided not to get a Covid vaccine despite turning 60 in 2021. Why is that?

Here are my nine reasons for not getting a Covid vaccine. I think most unvaccinated people, as well as people who were forced to get a Covid vaccine, or else lose their job or not be able to enter higher education or remain in the armed forces, can relate to one or more of these reasons. I'm sure that people have other reasons as well.

I'd like people who support Covid vaccine mandates to understand these reasons. I'd like them to know that people who refused Covid vaccination had important reasons before making their decision.

**Reason #1: Event 201**

Many people chose not to get vaccinated after learning about Event 201, which was a 3.5 hour meeting held in New York city to simulate what a coordinated pandemic response would look like in the event of an actual pandemic. It was held on October 18th 2019, a full 5 months before anyone had heard of Covid and was sponsored by The John Hopkins Center for Health Security, the World Economic Forum and the Gates Foundation.

Attendees at Event 201 included George Gao, the director of the Chinese CDC, Hasti Taghi, a vice president for NBC, Avril Haines, the former deputy director of the Central Intelligence -Agency, Chris Elias, a director of the Bill and Melinda Gates Foundation and Timothy Grant Evans, a former World Health Organization and Rockefeller Foundation official

Investigative journalist Jordan Schachtel listed those names of people attending (among others) in his eye-opening article **Event 201: organizers of WEF-Gates pre-Covid simulation warned of 'similar pandemic in the future' - A smoking gun?** It is worthy of reading.

On the Event 201 website we read:
*"The exercise illustrated areas where public/private partnerships will be necessary during the response to a severe pandemic."*

The World Economic Forum, established in 1971, brings together the billionaire class to, in their own words: "...*shape global, regional and industry agendas*" and focus on: "*developing solutions to the world's greatest challenges… to shape the future... to ensure strategic decision-making on the most pressing world issues*."

Members of the World Economic Forum include Pfizer, Moderna, the Gates Foundation, healthcare chains and many other global companies, including high tech.

Anthony Fauci is directly connected to John Hopkins University, which, again, sponsored Event 201. He has spoken at John Hopkins numerous times, including in November 2020 when he delivered a keynote address exploring the pandemic response options including the production of Covid vaccines.

If you want to know about Dr. Fauci's illustrious past, please read Robert F Kennedy Jr's book "The Real Anthony Fauci"

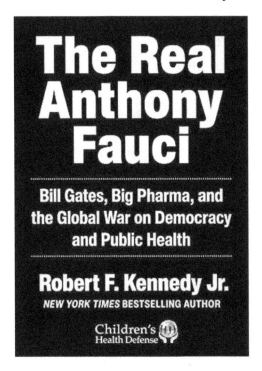

I have come to believe that the purpose of the World Economic Forum and many of its partners, including the Gates Foundation, is social engineering.

Not trusting social engineers is one of the primary reasons many people refused to take a Covid vaccine. Was it just a coincidence that the crafters of the worldwide Covid response were the same people that had participated in Event 201?

On the topic of not trusting unelected groups, a doctor who goes by the name "A Midwestern Doctor" wrote in his October 20th 2022 article **Who Owns the CDC**:

*"In democratic republics, it should not be possible for unelected groups to forcefully dictate the lives of citizens without those policies being legalized by the legislative process. Unfortunately, our bureaucracy has bypassed that process by allowing committees (whose members are appointed rather than being elected democratically) to craft "guidelines" (as this is the limit of their authority), and then have the rest of the government (and media) treat those guidelines as laws. Unfortunately, the members of these committees tend to be individuals who have been bribed and inevitably arrive at conclusions that support their sponsors."*

**Reason #2 Many Unvaccinated people have had Covid already**
We were taught in school that if a person gets sick and recovers from a viral infection, that they are immune to that virus when it circulates in a community later. When I was a child, neighbors would have chicken pox parties because they wanted their children to get infected in order to develop immunity against the chicken pox.

The traditional vaccines most of us took as children, like for Polio, Rubella, the Mumps and Measles gave us a very tiny piece of the virus and our immune systems learned how to deal with it later if or when we encountered the real virus. (Covid vaccines are different.)

Many people got Covid in 2020. I got Covid just before Christmas 2021 on a trip to Las Vegas to get some sunshine.  (Western Washington state winters are very gloomy.)

Everyone was masked in Las Vegas, as it was mandated, and I was wearing a mask, social distancing, washing my hands often and taking vitamin D3 and C, Quercetin and zinc. I take Quercetin and zinc occasionally when I know I'll be around people or when I start to feel sick.

There are two places I likely got Covid (I can't know for sure). The first place was a crowded buffet line. Over 60 masked people were standing together in an alcove for 40 minutes with no ventilation.

The next place was on a bus ride to and from the Grand Canyon where I took my step-daughter and my Japanese home stay daughter.

My Covid infection started with a bad headache, followed by a fever, a runny nose, a cough, loss of smell and taste, and exhaustion. It resulted in heavy symptoms for 2 days, and milder symptoms for 3 or 4 more days. The most prominent symptom was exhaustion. I was extremely tired for 5 or 6 days. I stayed home 2 weeks after symptoms presented because I didn't want to infect anyone.

Before 2020, if I had had that exact same illness start on a Saturday or Sunday, I would have taken Monday off work. Before 2020, I would have taken over the counter medicine to relieve my symptoms and drunk coffee to stay awake. I am happy that I survived a Covid infection. I'm sure it gives me some level of protection against SARS-CoV-2 and its variants. The reason many of us declined Covid vaccination is because of the immunity we gained from recovering from a Covid infection.

## Reason #3: Assessing our personal risk

As mentioned in the last chapter, many of us decided against taking a Covid vaccine because we figured out our personal risk of a death involving Covid.

The following chart is from an Illinois newspaper published on November 18th 2020. It showed the chance a person infected with Covid has of dying based on their age. From charts like this and by analyzing numbers on various websites, like the CDC, and Our World in Data, we assessed our own probability of death.

### CDC's COVID-19 Infection Fatality Rate

| Infection Fatality Rate (IFR) | Probability of death | Probability of survival |
|---|---|---|
| 1 out of 34,000 for **ages 0 to 19** | 0.003% | 99.997% |
| 1 out of 5,000 for **ages 20 to 49** | 0.020% | 99.980% |
| 1 out of 200 for **ages 50 to 69** | 0.500% | 99.500% |
| 1 out of 20 for **ages 70 and up** | 5.400% | 94.600% |

Source: U.S. Centers for Disease Control and Prevention        WIREPOINTS

The infection fatality rate shows the relationship between infections and death. For example, according to the chart, if you are between the ages of 20-49, for every 5000 people who get infected with the Covid-19 virus, 1 person will die. This equates to 0.02% dying… and 99.98% surviving.

Almost everyone who gets infected with the Covid-19 virus survives, even those over the age of 70. Again, the risk of a Covid-related death is largely dependent on age, underlying health, level of obesity, vitamin D levels and the strength of a person's immune system. People should have the freedom to take a personal risk assessment. Medical procedures should not be mandated.

Doctors should be free to work with their patients and not be under the control of Big Pharma, billionaires and the World Economic Forum or the CDC.

As an aside, one reason many Americans doubted what they were hearing about the safety and efficacy of Covid vaccines is that the US government seems to have been taken over by the billionaire class and drug company lobbyists. If government leaders in the US really cared about regular people in the US, would we see such horrible problems like increasing rates of homelessness, hunger, a very weak social safety net, high levels of price inflation, no accountability when the powerful break the law, stories of war that aren't complete, a lack of honesty, etc?

It seems that the vast majority of people we elect to the highest levels of power in the US, regardless of their political party, are morally compromised to some degree. So, when they were suddenly concerned about vaccinating all of us because they cared, I was skeptical. I didn't like nor trust the people pushing us to take an experimental shot.

### Reason #4: A bad experience with pharmaceuticals or the healthcare system
Many unvaccinated people have had negative, if not traumatic, experiences with prescription drugs and/ or the healthcare system. As a result, they have developed a combination of fear, wariness and skepticism when asked to take a medication or undergo a medical procedure. They don't do either thing easily.

When I was 13 years old, I suffered from a digestive disorder which stumped the doctors. It started suddenly and lasted for 15 months. They called it ileitis, inflammation of the digestive tract. Basically, for 15 months every time I ate, I had intense pain and the food left me quickly.

Because of not being able to digest food and absorb nutrients, I had to be given nutrients intravenously. For 15 months I took a lot of medications and treatments, but nothing relieved my symptoms or the incredible pain I suffered every time I ate even a tiny bit, like ¼ of a cracker. At 5'8" I got down to 105 pounds. My mom took me to the hospital a lot. At one point the doctors suggested I get surgery to remove some of my intestine. I said, "Absolutely not, I'd rather die." And odd as it may seem, my mom, who I know loved me dearly, didn't argue the point.

A couple of months after the appointment when the doctor had suggested surgery, the doctor told my mom and me that he didn't know what else to do for me. I was 14 years old and upon hearing the doctor's words, I saw sudden and complete darkness. I was relieved to know that this sickness was over in a sense but I felt completely alone. No more doctors.

My mom and I went home, and I threw away all of my bottles of medication. Later that evening I announced to my parents, "I'm going to bed and If God wants me alive, I'll live. If he wants me to go, I'll go. It has to be one way or the other." My parents cried, and I felt strengthened in my resolve to either die or stay alive and I went to bed.

I was raised in a secular family and had never gone to church. But I still felt that there was a God. I think my parent's cried mostly because they loved me. But I think they also cried because I showed faith, which both of them seemed to have abandoned earlier in their lives. I went to bed and when I woke up early the next morning with the sun, I felt a gentle happiness and I knew I was going to be OK. I opened my bedroom door to find my mom standing right outside of it. "Are you ready to try to eat something?" she asked. I ate ¼ of a cracker and felt fine. I was back to normal after about 2 weeks.

Isn't it reasonable for people like me who have had negative experiences with the healthcare system or prescription drugs to be skeptical of Covid vaccines and to do research?

People who have had traumatic experiences with the healthcare industry and pharmaceuticals don't put anything in their body that is questionable. They have to know what exactly is going on.

**Reason #5: Firmly held spiritual beliefs**
Some of us chose not to get vaccinated because we are religious or spiritual. We try to live according to what we feel is God's will for us. I've found that many people, religious or not, got a feeling not to take a Covid vaccine. I heard a voice in my head say "It's not for you" when I read about the vaccine in late 2020.

Is it reasonable not to do something when a strong feeling inside of you gives you a clear message not to do it? I think nearly everyone can relate to not taking a certain job, or not moving to a certain place or not going out with a certain person again simply because of having a strong feeling telling them not to. It's intuition, and we all have it.

**Reason #6: The Covid vaccines come with risks**
The sixth reason that we decided not to take a Covid vaccine is we found out that Covid vaccines come with risks. There are many Covid vaccine associated injuries that have been reported, like myocarditis (inflammation of the heart), permanent disability, miscarriages, reproductive issues and deaths. Of course, these injuries and deaths could simply have been coincidental, but they were all reported shortly after a person getting a Covid vaccine. The VAERS reports also refer to the Covid vaccine.

Many people developed myocarditis soon after getting a Covid vaccine. This is a serious matter. Myocarditis can lead to heart attacks and sudden death from a heart attack. And it's a known risk that comes with Covid vaccination.

That said, in this November 11th 2021 AP article we read:

## Social media posts misrepresent myocarditis risks

By TERRENCE FRASER    November 11, 2021

*"Everything we know about this vaccine is that it is a very well tolerated vaccine that has an exceptionally low rate of adverse events." Cooper said. "Many millions of people have received the mRNA COVID vaccines. And of all of those, there have been less than 1,000 reported cases of myocarditis in hundreds of millions of vaccines."*

As of August 13, 2022, less than a year after this article was published, there have been over 8,700 reported cases of myocarditis and pericarditis in the US reported to VAERS and I'm sure way more than that number have gone unreported, all related to "very well tolerated" Covid vaccines. People who remain unvaccinated don't want to assume risks. They'd rather take the risk of Covid infection than a Covid vaccine.

**Reason #7: The Covid vaccines and boosters don't stop transmission or infection and they don't prevent death.**

Do you remember when we were told: **"When people are vaccinated, they can feel safe that they are not going to get infected"** -Anthony Fauci, May 17th 2021

Fauci told a lie. Vaccinated people still get infected, transmit the Corona virus and also sometimes die.

Let's revisit the Washington State report on breakthrough deaths. On the Washington State Dept of Health website there is a report called **SARS-CoV-2 Vaccine Breakthrough Surveillance and Case Information Resource**. In this report the Washington State Department of Health tells us the number of vaccinated people who got a Covid infection and the number of vaccinated people who died. The report is updated monthly.

Here is an image of the Washington State Dept of Health numbers from January 17th 2021 to July 30th 2022:

**At a Glance (data from January 17, 2021 - July 30, 2022)**
- 670,119 SARS-CoV-2 vaccine breakthrough cases have been identified in Washington State. Of these breakthrough cases:
  - 15% reported symptoms
  - 3% were hospitalized
  - 0.4% died of COVID-related illness

Between Jan 17, 2021 to July 30, 2022, there were 670,119 Covid-19 vaccine breakthrough infections, meaning that approximately 12% of all vaccinated people in Washington state got a Covid infection.

On top of that, a total of **2,979 vaccinated Washingtonians had deaths involving Covid.** In the image below note the age range in deaths (age 15-106). The median (average) age was 79, which means most breakthrough deaths are occurring in older populations.

COVID-19 deaths among SARS-CoV-2 breakthrough cases in Washington State

January 17, 2021 - July 30, 2022

Among breakthrough cases from this surveillance period **2,979** have died of COVID-related illness.

The age range of deceased cases was 15 - 106 years (median 79 years).

Here are the number of deaths involving Covid January-July 2022 in WA state. (This is a screen shot from the CDC):

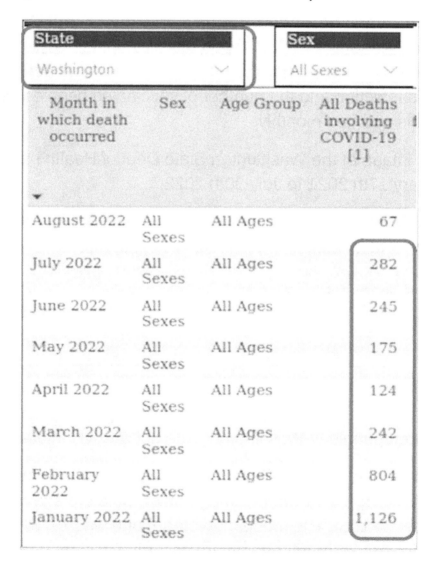

| State | | | | Sex | |
|---|---|---|---|---|---|
| Washington | | | | All Sexes | |

| Month in which death occurred | Sex | Age Group | All Deaths involving COVID-19 [1] |
|---|---|---|---|
| August 2022 | All Sexes | All Ages | 67 |
| July 2022 | All Sexes | All Ages | 282 |
| June 2022 | All Sexes | All Ages | 245 |
| May 2022 | All Sexes | All Ages | 175 |
| April 2022 | All Sexes | All Ages | 124 |
| March 2022 | All Sexes | All Ages | 242 |
| February 2022 | All Sexes | All Ages | 804 |
| January 2022 | All Sexes | All Ages | 1,126 |

According to the CDC, a total of **2,998** Covid related deaths occurred in Washington state from January through July 2022. Compare that number to the number of Covid breakthrough deaths in fully vaccinated people (**2,979**). The number of vaccinated who died since the vaccine roll out was nearly the same as the total number of Covid related deaths in the first 7 months of 2022. Covid vaccines don't prevent infection... and they don't always prevent death. We have been terribly misled.

# Reason 8 - Natural Skeptics

Reason number eight that many people refused to get a Covid vaccine is that many unvaccinated people are naturally skeptical. They don't automatically trust authority. Obviously, skeptical people were curious about Covid vaccines when they were told to take one. They did research and decided against it.

On April 27th 2022, Igor Chudov, mathematician and business owner, wrote an article entitled **mRNA Vaccine Skeptics are the True Critical Thinkers.** In it he wonders what made the unvaccinated decide against getting a Covid vaccine and asked readers to give their reasons (bolding was done by Chudov.):

*"Regarding mRNA "Covid vaccines": anyone who would think for a minute, would realize that* **there was not a way to know for sure that vaccines were safe and effective, simply because not enough time has passed.**

*Similarly, anyone could see that the masterminds behind the lockdowns and vaccinations, the billionaires behind the scenes, and the corrupt governments, all ensured that any dissent would be silenced.*

*Thus,* **the purported consensus did not, in fact, exist at all.**

*The minority of people saw through that, decided accordingly, and refused vaccination.*

**Who was that? You, my readers.**

*What made you decide this?*

*I am sure that there were just as many reasons as people here.* **The main factor is that you all took a few minutes to think about it critically.**

*You were independently minded and decided to think for yourselves.*

*-Was it your general distrust of the government?*

*-Was is your deep knowledge of virology and molecular biology?*

*-Was it your experience with wheeling and dealing, exposure to scams and knowing how con men operate?*

*-Was it your ability to think independently without needing people to agree with you?*

*Even those who took the shots, and saw the light later, are critical thinkers. What is important is seeing the light — not necessarily the timing of when you saw the light.*

*To those who survived* **The Global Asch Experiment,** *congratulations. Please share what made you hold out, below —* **Why did you NOT get the shot?"**

So, against the backdrop of having gone through a thought process and then deciding not to take a Covid vaccine, the unvaccinated got this scolding from President Joe Biden on September 9, 2021:

*"We've been patient, but our patience is wearing thin."*

With all due respect President Biden, our patience has also worn thin. We studied Covid vaccines and made an informed decision for ourselves not to take one. Please leave us alone. We don't appreciate your threatening and fear-based tone.

**Finally Reason #9**...Pfizer exec admits that he's not certain if the Pfizer Covid vaccine will stop transmission.

In 2020 and 2021 many people who chose not to take a Covid vaccine were also reading how it was uncertain if Covid vaccines would prevent transmission. From the December 4th 2020 article **Pfizer CEO admits he is 'not certain' their COVID-19 shot will prevent vaccinated people from spreading the virus...** we read:

*"Pfizer's corona virus jab may not prevent vaccinated people from spreading corona virus, the firm's chairman admitted this week.*

*'I think that's something that needs to be examined. We're not certain about that right now,' said Albert Bourla, when asked by Dateline's Lester Holt about whether the shot would prevent transmission during the interview, which aired Thursday night."*

In fact, Bourla admitted that Pfizer hadn't tested whether or not trial participants were still able to transmit the virus.

**Later in October 2022, Pfizer admitted to the European Parliament that their vaccines weren't designed to stop transmission.**

Despite these nine reasons, the government, schools, the military and many workplaces mandate that we get vaccinated even if we don't want to.

Don't we also get to say "My body, my choice"?

If you allow the government to push vaccine mandates now, what will you allow them to mandate next?

In the next chapter we will talk about vaccination rates in the US in more detail and look at an arduous vaccine exemption form.

# 6... Covid Vaccination rates and an example of a vaccine exemption form

*"The other day someone I know posted a quote from the poet Mary Oliver, "Listen, are you breathing just a little, and calling it a life?" And I almost began to cry. I kept thinking of how scared I've been, how scared many of us have been during these years of the pandemic. And of course, it's not just the pandemic, so many overwhelming fears. I read that quote and I suddenly longed for breath. For relief. For the end of fear."*
— Ada Limon (1976-) is an American poet. She wrote 6 poetry books. On July 12th 2022, she was named the 24th Poet Laureate of the United States by the Librarian of Congress.

In this chapter my goal is to show you the cumulative rate of people getting vaccinated in the US through September 12$^{th}$ and an example of a Covid vaccine exemption form. I hope you will agree that forcing people to fill out arduous forms to protect their health from an experimental drug is wrong and a complete invasion of privacy.

The fear during the Covid-era has been intense. At times it has felt otherworldly and palpable. In the minds of many people, getting vaccinated meant we would be able to put the Covid pandemic behind us and the fear would end.

When did people start taking Covid vaccines in the US? From Our World in Data we see the largest share of the population received their first Covid vaccine by April 2021.(I inserted lines to show approximately when 2021 and 2022 started.)

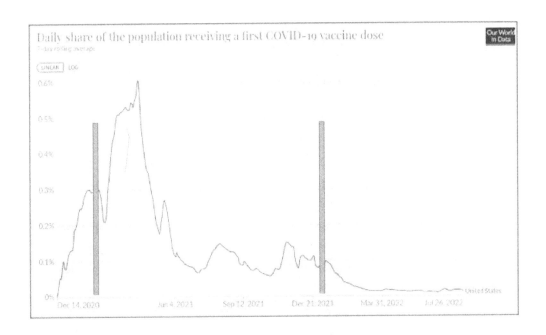

Daily share of the population receiving a first COVID-19 vaccine dose
7-day rolling average

We can assume that people took their second dose of the vaccine two weeks after they took their first dose. However, some people took just one dose of a Pfizer or Moderna vaccine and decided not to take a second dose.

Again, according to the CDC, by June 24th 2021 the fully vaccinated rates were:

| Age | % Fully Vaccinated |
|---|---|
| 5-11 | 0.4% |
| 12-17 | 26.3% |
| 18-24 | 41.3% |
| 25-49 | 50.4% |
| 50-64 | 66.7% |
| 65+ | 81% |

Looking at the **Our World in Data** chart again, notice the increase in people receiving their initial vaccine at the end of June 2021. That increase coincided with college and university students and teachers and college staff being mandated to get vaccinated (2 Pfizer or Moderna, 1 Johnson and Johnson) before going to back to school in August or September 2021. Again, here are the vaccination rates as of September 12, 2022 according to the CDC data tracker:

| Age | % Fully Vaccinated |
|---|---|
| Under 2 | 0.9% |
| 2-4 | 1.7% |
| 5-11 | 31.1% |
| 12-17 | 60.5% |
| 18-24 | 64.9% |
| 25-49 | 70.5% |
| 50-64 | 82.3% |
| 65+ | 92.1% |

Nearly everyone over the age of 65 is "fully vaccinated" in terms of having taken the first two shots. Yet, hardly anyone is taking boosters. According to the article **Experts warn of King County COVID surge, few people have gotten updated booster** (October 5th 2022) we learn that in King County (Washington state where Seattle is located) **fewer than 10% of all eligible people have taken a booster**.

When asked about the risk of Covid, one person is quoted as saying "I feel like it's going away." It seems like that to me too, AND I think the popularity of Covid vaccines is going away too. Even with the efficacy and safety of Covid vaccines being highly questionable, we have colleges, universities, the US military and some jobs continue to demand people take a Covid vaccine. It just doesn't make sense.

Vaccine mandates have caused an unbelievable amount of stress in the US population. Are the mandates really necessary for public health? What are the exact reasons for the mandates when the vaccines did not make our death rate go down and do not prevent infection, transmission and death?

Many people seek vaccine exemptions. Vaccine exemption requests are not always granted and are arduous in nature. Consider these questions on a vaccine exemption form used by New York University (NYU) (my underlining):

*"This form must be completed to apply for a religious exemption to New York University's immunization requirements. The request must be based on a sincere and genuine religious belief that is contrary to the practice of immunization. <u>Please note that medical, scientific, political, philosophical, ethical, or otherwise secular objections to immunization do not justify an exemption…</u>"*

(My underlining because that statement is outrageous.- If your objections aren't religious in nature, but are otherwise valid, you are out of luck. How many religions actually prohibit vaccination? These people are on a power trip, especially in light of what we now know about Covid vaccines.)

Here is more of NYU's vaccine exemption form:

*"In the area provided below, please write your statement clearly and legibly. The statement must address all of the following elements:*

☐ *Explain in your own words why you are requesting this religious exemption.*

☐ *Describe with specificity the religious principles that guide your objection to immunization. You should explain how your religious belief requires you not to be immunized.*

☐ *Have you taken other vaccinations previously?*

☐ *If your belief relates to substances in your body, what other commonly used substances does your belief not permit in your body?*

☐ *If your belief relates to development and/or testing that involved fetal cells, do you use medications such as Advil (ibuprofen), acetaminophen (Tylenol), or other medications that used fetal cell lines in development or testing?*

☐ *Indicate which immunizations you are opposed to by checking the boxes below. If you are not opposed to all immunizations, please indicate in your response the religious basis that prohibits particular immunizations.*

*All immunizations*

*COVID-19*

*Measles, Mumps, Rubella (MMR)*

*Meningococcal Meningitis*

*This statement must describe the beliefs in sufficient detail to allow NYU to determine that (1) the beliefs are truly religious in nature and (2) the beliefs are genuinely and sincerely held. (Then there are two pages of lines on which students write their request essay followed by more directions.)*

---

*You should attach to this form additional written pages or other materials that support your request, which may include:*

☐ *Where your belief relates to membership in an organized religion whose doctrines are contrary to immunization, you should submit a letter from an authorized representative of your religious*

---

*organization, or other literature from such organization, explaining the doctrines that prohibit immunization. Please note that a clergy or similar letter is not required, but may be helpful when the clergy has a personal relationship with you. Form letters or letters from clergy you do not know are generally unhelpful;*

*☐ Other writings or sources upon which you relied in formulating religious beliefs that prohibit immunization;*

*☐ A copy of any statements to healthcare providers or officials at other schools explaining the religious basis for refusing immunization; and*

*☐ Any other documents or other information you wish to provide that demonstrate a sincerely and genuinely held religious objection to immunization.*

*Please sign in the space provided below:*

*I hereby affirm the truthfulness of the foregoing statement.*

*Signature of Student (if 18 or over) Date*

*Signature of Parent or Guardian (if under 18) Date*

*Please submit this statement to the Director of Operations, Student Health Center by uploading your statement on the Student Health Center portal at shcportal.nyu.edu."*

I wonder how many students and college staff have had to construct elaborate lies in order to fill out vaccine exemption forms like this. I wonder how many students decided against going to NYU and to the other colleges and universities that mandate Covid vaccination. I wonder how many staff have quit.

I'd like to see a similar application that people have to fill out before getting a Covid vaccine with questions such as:

1- Are you aware the Covid vaccines do not stop transmission, infection and may not stop death?

2- Are you aware that you are taking a risk and that serious vaccine injuries like x, y, and z have occurred?

3- Are you aware that x number of people in your age group out of a population of y have died from a Covid infection and that your chance of dying is approximately z% if you get a Covid infection?

4- Are you aware that we don't know the long-term effects of Covid vaccination?

5- Are you aware that you could …. and …. and …. to improve your immune system and your health?

Do you still want one now?

If people still want a Covid vaccine, they should absolutely be able to get one. If people don't want a Covid vaccine, they absolutely should have the right not to get one. No coercion.

**How many people are boosted in the US?**
By August 2022 about 36 booster shots have been administered per 100 people. This doesn't mean that 36 people are boosted out of 100 because some people have had more than one booster.

The chart below is from **Our World In Data:**

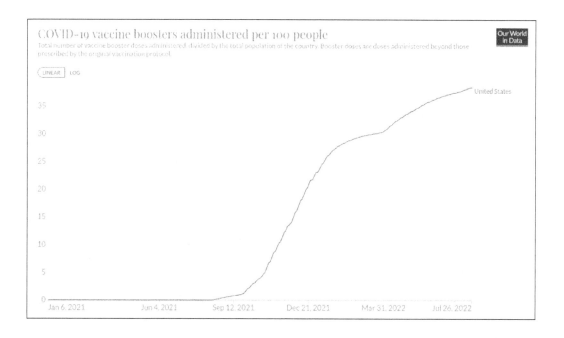

COVID-19 vaccine boosters administered per 100 people

Total number of vaccine booster doses administered, divided by the total population of the country. Booster doses are doses administered beyond those prescribed by the original vaccination protocol.

Boosting began in early September 2021. Since then, it seems that the majority of Americans who had taken their initial series of Covid vaccines refused to be boosted. As we previously noted, less than 10 percent of people are current on Covid booster shots.

Whether or not to take a Covid vaccine or a booster should be up to each person and coercion by means of being denied entrance to work, higher education and the military must end.

Do the desires of 1/3 of the US population that decided against getting the Covid vaccination not matter?

How about the 90% of us who have now decided not to get the booster shots?

In the next chapter we will look at corona viruses and the difficulty in developing a vaccine for a corona virus.

# 7... Corona viruses and the difficulty in making a corona virus vaccine

*"The healthy man does not torture others- generally it is the tortured who turn into torturers."*

- Carl Jung (1875-1961) was a Swiss psychiatrist who talked a lot about the collective unconscious (all people united on a level of consciousness), archetypes (parts of the past in us) and personality types- he developed the theory or extroversion and introversion.

In this chapter my goal is to explain what corona viruses are, how they work in the body and the difficulty in making a corona virus vaccine. I hope that you will question their efficacy and wonder why they are mandated.

Most of us hadn't heard of the Corona virus until the Covid-era began in 2020. However, all of us have had a lot of contact with corona viruses already in our lives.

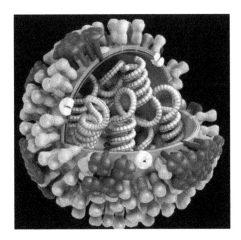

**A corona virus (author Doug Jordan, MA, USCDCP)**

The fact is that there are many kinds of corona viruses in the world and about 7 kinds affect humans. Corona viruses cause about 20% of all common colds. The human immune system has learned to respond to corona viruses because of having met so many.

Corona viruses all have spikes. They form a "crown" on the shell of the virus. (The word *corona* means *crown* in Latin.) The spikes help corona viruses enter your cells. The spikes come out of an envelope and inside of the envelope is RNA, which is genetic material.

After a corona virus enters your cell by using its spikes, the RNA takes control of your cell's machinery to replicate, make copies of itself. The copying process is done in a sneaky way because it occurs inside a double-membrane compartment that keeps the virus hidden from the cell.

When the replicated corona viruses leave a cell, they enter more cells and soon millions and billions more corona viruses are created. When a person's immune system recognizes what is happening, it starts an immune response and creates antibodies to fight the viruses. We get sick from a corona virus infection when the viral load – how much virus is in our bodies- overpowers the strength of our immune system.

It has been very interesting to me that since the start of the Covid pandemic that very few people in mainstream media, including the TV news and the newspapers, has talked much about how a person can improve his or her immune system to make it stronger and better able to fight infections.

Again, why haven't we been told repeatedly about the dangers of obesity and low vitamin D levels and how to strengthen our immune system?

I wonder (again) if any lives would have saved if we as a nation all Americans had gone on a health kick.

## Corona viruses and Mutations

You have heard of the word mutation. Corona viruses have a tendency to mutate (change). When they are busy make copies of themselves, replicating in the cells, sometimes a copy is made wrong. That is what a mutation is. According to Dr. Michael Yeadon, who was a chief scientist in drug discovery research and a VP at Pfizer for 20 years: *"… no variant is even close to evading immunity acquired by natural infection. It is because the human immune system recognizes 20–30 different structural motifs in the virus, yet requires only a handful to recall an effective immune memory."*

When I read Yeadon's words, I was happy I had had a Covid infection. From **Our World in Data** here are the mutations of SARS-CoV-2 in the US reported on August 1, 2022. The different variants of SARS-Cov-2 we've had include: Alpha, Beta, Gamma, Delta and members of the Omicron family. The mutations we are dealing with now are all of variations of the Omicron family.

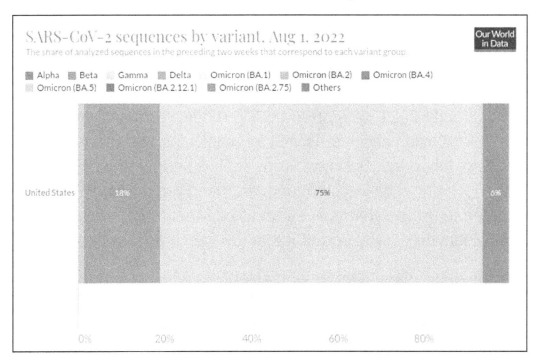

The diagram above shows us the Covid-19 variants that were in circulation among the population from the middle of July 2022 to August 1st 2022. 75% of people were getting infected with the Omicron variant BA 5. There were three Omicron variants circulating during those 2 weeks: BA 2.12.1, BA 2.75 and BA 5.

You might have got sick with BA 5 where you live and your friend in another state might have got infected with BA 4.

By the time you take a Covid vaccine, the exact corona virus mutation the vaccine was designed to fight has more than likely changed. Natural immunity is superior according to many doctors and scientists because it stops viruses even after they have mutated.

**The making and marketing of Covid vaccines**
I do understand that because we wanted to build herd immunity against SARS-CoV-2 in 2020, many people welcomed a Covid vaccine in 2021.

Covid vaccines were first made available and promoted to people over the age of 18, then for children age 5-17 and now they are offered to children 6 months old.

Starting in early 2021 we started seeing movie stars and famous people take Covid vaccines as well as politicians and other people in positions of influence. Soon we were seeing people on social media proudly declaring their vaccination status and urging others to get vaccinated to protect themselves and to do their part in protecting others. Meanwhile I was doubtful that the vaccine would even work.

In April of 2020, many doctors and scientists who were not allowed on mainstream media were already saying that developing a successful vaccine against SARS-CoV-2 would be very difficult. It had never been done successfully before despite trying.

In the following article from April 16th 2020, Dr. Ian Frazer, vaccinologist, explains why it is hard to make a Covid vaccine:

*"For those pinning their hopes on a COVID-19 vaccine to return life to normal, an Australian expert in vaccine development has a reality check — it probably won't happen soon. The reality is that this particular corona virus is posing challenges that scientists haven't dealt with before, according to Ian Frazer from the University of Queensland.*

*Professor Frazer was involved in the successful development of the vaccine for the human papilloma virus which causes cervical cancer — a vaccine which took years of work to develop. He said the challenge is that corona viruses have historically been hard to make safe vaccines for, partly because the virus infects the upper respiratory tract, which our immune system isn't great at protecting."*

Do we believe Professor Frazer or do we believe Anthony Fauci? What criteria does one use when deciding who to believe?

Let's revisit the Anthony Fauci promise:

**"When people are vaccinated, they can feel safe that they are not going to get infected"** - Anthony Fauci, May 17th 2021

By November 2021, I imagine much to Dr Fauci's disappointment, we found that the Covid vaccines lose effectiveness:

---

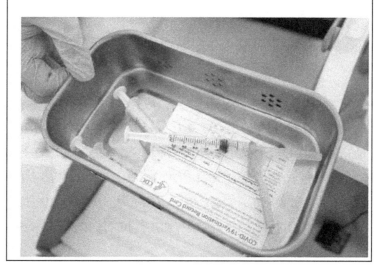

**Los Angeles Times**

Study shows dramatic decline in effectiveness of all three COVID-19 vaccines over time

From the LA Times on November 4th 2021 we read (my underlining):

*"As the Delta variant became the dominant strain of the corona virus across the United States, <u>all three COVID-19 vaccines available to Americans lost some of their protective power, with vaccine efficacy among a large group of veterans dropping between 35% and 85%,</u> according to a new study...*

*By the end of September, Moderna's two-dose COVID-19 vaccine, measured as 89% effective in March, was only 58% effective.*

*The effectiveness of shots made by Pfizer and BioNTech, which also employed two doses, <u>fell from 87% to 45% in the same period</u>.*

*And most strikingly, the protective power of Johnson & Johnson's single-dose vaccine <u>plunged from 86% to just 13% over those six months."</u>*

Covid vaccines were sold to us as the way to protect people from Covid infections and to build herd immunity so the Covid pandemic would end. Many people had thought that the Covid vaccines, like the vaccines they were familiar with, would offer long-lasting protection.

The truth is that the initial series of Covid vaccines people took in the first few months of 2021 have stopped working altogether by mid-2022. And many fully vaccinated people have been infected numerous times with Covid.

Dr. Theo Schetters, a highly respected vaccinologist in the Netherlands, talks about how many scientists knew at the beginning of the Covid vaccination campaign in 2021 that Covid vaccines wouldn't work as promised. Here is part of the interview he had with Dr Robert Malone, inventor of mRNA technology, on August 2nd 2022 (my underlining) :

*"The thing that we knew from the beginning, was that COVID (SARS-CoV-2) was a very mutating virus. So I always said, it's like you run with your syringe behind the virus, that's running away from you. And so you can never keep up with the mutations. And that is actually that's what we see now.*

*So also the Netherlands, the National Institute of Health has said that people that have been vaccinated twice with the original vaccine,* **that at this moment there is zero protection anymore***. So that's official result, that on the efficacy side (zero protection).*

*Then on the safety side, we also see problems. That's the most difficult part because* <u>*people (the government) do not want to talk about the safety. There's so many people that contact me because in the Netherlands, I'm some sort of famous. So I get emails and phone calls of people who have had very bad experiences after vaccination.*</u>

*And the sad thing is that, although these people obeyed the rules of the government and trusted them, now that they have these terrible side effects, the government doesn't want to listen. You know, they are just so neglected. We don't talk about it. And that's the situation at the moment."*

One thing I do know for sure about Covid vaccines is that they have made a ton of money for Pfizer, Moderna, Johnson & Johnson and their shareholders.

It seems to me that the many millions of people who have taken a Covid vaccine are actually participants in the world's biggest drug trial ever run.

In the next chapter we will learn more about Covid vaccine efficacy. How long does their protection actually last?

# 8... Covid Vaccine Efficacy

*"If the ladder is not leaning against the right wall, every step we take just gets us to the wrong place faster."*

-Stephen Covey (1932-2012) was an author and business man. He was famous for writing the best-selling book "The 7 Habits of Highly Successful People".

In this chapter my goal is to prove to you how ineffective Covid vaccines are. I hope you will agree that mandating people take a vaccine which doesn't work as promised is wrong.

It's August 2022, over a year and a half after the push to Covid vaccinate the entire population over the age of 18 (and since June 2022 the push to Covid vaccinate babies over the age of six months). Are we sure Covid vaccines prevent transmission and infection like we were promised? Do they prevent death? Are they safe?

President Joe Biden was vaccinated and boosted, and he has had two Covid infections. Here's what a man named Ian Miller said on Twitter:

Ian Miller
@ianmSC

With four vaccination doses, treatment with Pfizer's Paxlovid, supposedly "strict isolation procedures" and continued masking, Joe Biden tested positive for COVID yet again today

How can anyone support continued mandates after this?
outkick.com/joe-biden-test...

♡ 190     ↻ 820     ♡ 2.9K

We had been told in 2021 that that Covid vaccines would bring us herd immunity if enough people got vaccinated. However the messaging changed when in early 2022 we were told that the purpose of Covid vaccines was only to prevent severe infection and death. Dr. Deborah Birx was the White House's Covid response coordinator under President Donald Trump (2020-2021). She is also a specialist in HIV/AIDS immunology, vaccine research, and global health. Birx admitted she had known that COVID-19 vaccines were not going to protect against infection on the July 22nd 2022 Fox News program **Your World**:

*"I knew these vaccines were not going to protect against infection. And I think we overplayed the vaccines and it made people then worry that it's not going to protect against severe disease and hospitalization. It will. But let's be very clear: 50% of the people who died from the Omicron surge were older, vaccinated."*

Dr Birx would you say that the people in the United States have been:

a. misled

b. lied to… or

c. deceived?

**Studies on Covid vaccine efficacy**
Let's turn to studies which show that Covid vaccines lose efficacy over time, and don't stop transmission or infection. The Brownstone Institute compiled a list of 16 Covid vaccine efficacy studies. Here are short summaries of 3 of those studies:

**1- Study in Sweden** - Effectiveness of the Pfizer vaccine against infection decreased progressively from 92% at day 15-30 to 47% at day 121-180, and from day 211 onward no effectiveness could be detected.

**2- Study in Qatar** - Pfizer efficacy against severe and fatal disease, in the 85-95% range at least until 6 months after the second dose. However, the efficacy against infection waned down to around 30% at 15-19 weeks after the second dose.

**3- Study in the US** - fully vaccinated individuals with breakthrough infections have peak viral load similar to unvaccinated cases and can efficiently transmit infection in household settings, including to fully vaccinated contacts.

Covid vaccines are a new kind of vaccine never used before on millions of people. We were pushed to take them and promised miracles, but it turns out we've been consistently lied to.

On October 5, 2022, another study was released of more than 90,000 people in California comparing people who got 3 doses of the Moderna vaccine to people who were unvaccinated (no doses of any Covid Vaccine). Figure 2 on Page 30 of this study confirmed that **those with 3 doses of the Moderna vaccine (2 initial shots and one booster) were 25% to 27% more likely to get an infection (test positive) than those who were unvaccinated.**

The study called this result **"negative effectiveness"** (i.e., where the vaccinated have a higher infection rate than the unvaccinated). Vaccine effectiveness against infection was negative within five months (150 days) at minus-25%, meaning there were 25% more infections in the vaccinated than in the unvaccinated.

The results are shown below. The lowest figure was nearly minus-27%.

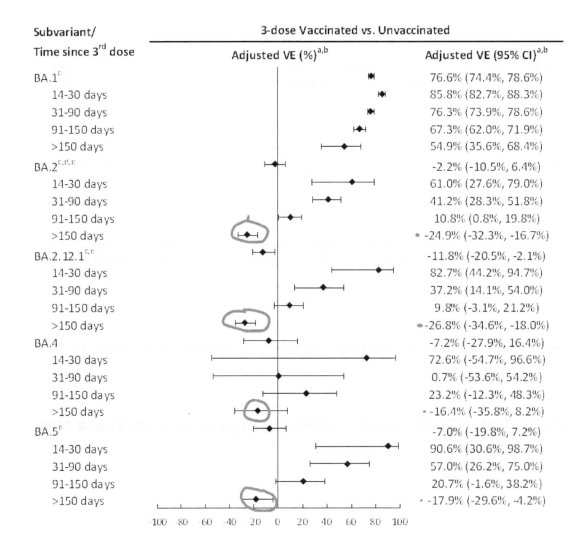

| Subvariant/ Time since 3rd dose | 3-dose Vaccinated vs. Unvaccinated | |
| --- | --- | --- |
| | Adjusted VE (%)[a,b] | Adjusted VE (95% CI)[a,b] |
| BA.1[c] | | 76.6% (74.4%, 78.6%) |
| 14-30 days | | 85.8% (82.7%, 88.3%) |
| 31-90 days | | 76.3% (73.9%, 78.6%) |
| 91-150 days | | 67.3% (62.0%, 71.9%) |
| >150 days | | 54.9% (35.6%, 68.4%) |
| BA.2[c,d,e] | | -2.2% (-10.5%, 6.4%) |
| 14-30 days | | 61.0% (27.6%, 79.0%) |
| 31-90 days | | 41.2% (28.3%, 51.8%) |
| 91-150 days | | 10.8% (0.8%, 19.8%) |
| >150 days | | -24.9% (-32.3%, -16.7%) |
| BA.2.12.1[c,e] | | -11.8% (-20.5%, -2.1%) |
| 14-30 days | | 82.7% (44.2%, 94.7%) |
| 31-90 days | | 37.2% (14.1%, 54.0%) |
| 91-150 days | | 9.8% (-3.1%, 21.2%) |
| >150 days | | -26.8% (-34.6%, -18.0%) |
| BA.4 | | -7.2% (-27.9%, 16.4%) |
| 14-30 days | | 72.6% (-54.7%, 96.6%) |
| 31-90 days | | 0.7% (-53.6%, 54.2%) |
| 91-150 days | | 23.2% (-12.3%, 48.3%) |
| >150 days | | -16.4% (-35.8%, 8.2%) |
| BA.5[e] | | -7.0% (-19.8%, 7.2%) |
| 14-30 days | | 90.6% (30.6%, 98.7%) |
| 31-90 days | | 57.0% (26.2%, 75.0%) |
| 91-150 days | | 20.7% (-1.6%, 38.2%) |
| >150 days | | -17.9% (-29.6%, -4.2%) |

Another study from Sweden published in the Lancet on September 20, 2022 also showed negative vaccine effectiveness against Omicron, this time for two doses and after just 15 weeks, with the trend moving deep into negative territory over time (see chart on next page).

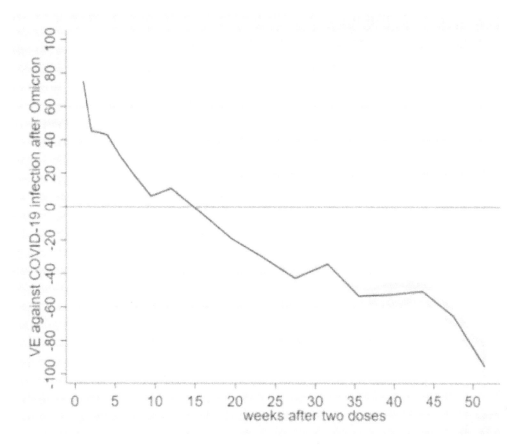

The fact that the negative effectiveness of the Covid vaccine approaches 100 percent over time (in the above case after about 50 weeks) would not be surprising to anyone who understand the natural immune system. The natural immune system offers years of protection. Therefore, we would expect that after many weeks nearly all infections would occur among the vaccinated. This is also what we saw in the Canada study which we discussed in Chapter 2.

Let's turn to New Zealand, where nearly all adults are fully vaccinated and there were increases in Covid cases and deaths.

**New Zealand- An example of the vaccine response to Covid not working**

Here is a Reuters news headline from July 22, 2022:
**"New Zealand COVID death rate at record level."**

---

The next three charts that show the results of mass vaccination in New Zealand's come from **Our World in Data.**

**Chart #1 – Vaccination rates in New Zealand**

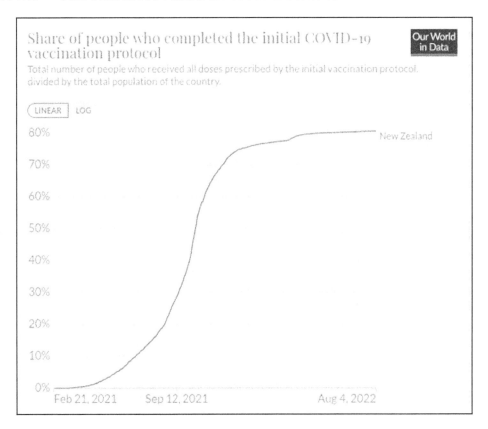

By Nov 8th 2021, 70% of New Zealand's total population had completed the  initial vaccine series (or protocol as the image says). On August 4th 2022 a full 80% of New Zealanders completed their initial series. That equates to 30% of 5-11 year olds and over 90% of everyone else

**Chart #2- Covid cases per million in New Zealand**

If Covid vaccines worked as we were promised in 2021, the huge increases in Covid cases in New Zealand wouldn't have happened.

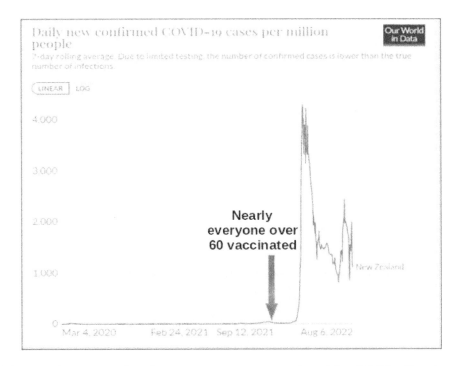

If Covid vaccines worked as we were promised in 2021, the huge increases in Covid deaths in NZ wouldn't have happened either.

## Chart #3- Deaths in New Zealand

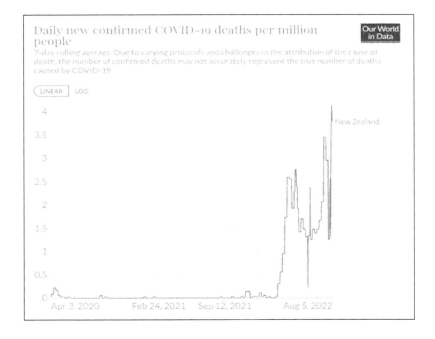

There were very few deaths in New Zealand until the first quarter of 2022. Note that the Y-axis refers to the number of people 0-4 and the title of the chart is deaths per million. So despite the steep upward trend, in light of the total population of New Zealand, very few people were dying. That said, these deaths likely occurred in the vaccinated population.

I wonder if all of the people who favor mandating Covid vaccines to go to school, get a job or join the armed forces are as arrogant as Dr. Fauci was in this statement:

*"Attacks on me, quite frankly, are attacks on science. … So if you are trying to, you know, get at me as a public health official and scientist, you're really attacking not only Dr. Anthony Fauci, you're attacking science … You have to be asleep not to see that."*

- Anthony Fauci, June 9, 2021

In the next chapter we will look at how mRNA vaccines work.

# 9... How do mRNA vaccines work?

*"The spike protein, which is both a part of the Covid-19 virus and is produced in our bodies after inoculation, can circulate around our bodies causing damage to cells, tissues, and organs. We do not know how long spike proteins stay in the body, however this guide is designed to reduce the load."*

- The Spike Protein Detox Guide was created in the fall of 2021 in response to the recognition that the spike proteins created in a vaccinated person's body circulate throughout the body and can possibly cause damage. It is a guide on how to reduce the load of spike proteins.

In this chapter my goal is to explain how the CDC says mRNA vaccines work in the body and how they changed their mind about how they work. I hope you will see the experimental nature of these vaccines and understand why a huge number of people have refused to take one because of the mRNA and spike proteins.

Moderna and Pfizer are mRNA vaccines. mRNA vaccines use a new technology and they are not like traditional vaccines. Everyone knew they were experimental, but many people were trusting and eager to get fully vaccinated. All Covid vaccines were given approval under emergency use authorization. Part of gaining emergency use authorization required proving that no other treatment options to Covid-19 existed. From the FDA website (my underlining):

*"(The) FDA may authorize unapproved medical products to be used in an emergency to diagnose, treat, or prevent serious or life-threatening diseases caused by chemical, biological, radiological, and nuclear threat agents when certain criteria are met, including <u>there are no adequate, approved, and available alternatives.</u>"*

Ivermectin and other therapeutics to fight Covid were not discussed in mainstream media and were, in fact, demonized because if they had been proven effective, the Covid vaccines wouldn't have been given emergency use authorization. Covid vaccines were indeed experimental, but we were assured that they were "safe and effective" despite no long-term data.

Oddly, many Democrats in power said that they wouldn't take a Covid vaccine developed under the Trump administration, but once Biden was in office, they promoted the same vaccines that they had refused earlier. I didn't understand that. I also didn't understand why everyone assumed I was a Republican or right wing for not taking one.

### mRNA Vaccines

The CDC has this image on their website to show us how the mRNA vaccines work. I will summarize what the information says in the image. Then we will look at what some doctors and scientists are saying about mRNA vaccines.

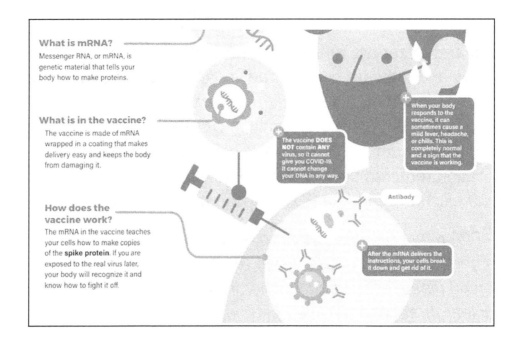

**Summarizing the CDC image above:**

The Pfizer and Moderna Covid vaccines contain messenger RNA, (mRNA). RNA is genetic material which is enclosed in a lipid packet (lipid is like fat; it doesn't dissolve in water). The mRNA, teaches your cells how to make copies of spike proteins, like the spikes on the Corona virus. After getting a Covid vaccine, there ends up being billions of spike proteins traveling throughout your body. Your body comes to understand those spikes as foreign, and creates antibodies to fight them.

Your body is literally creating the spikes that they are training your immune system to fight. The goal is that when you are exposed to spike proteins in real life, your immune system will know how to mount a defense, which will prevent a serious Covid infection and death.(Spike protein is the pathologic (makes you sick) component of the Covid-19 virus.)

According to the CDC, mRNA vaccines don't give you Covid, and minor side effects like fever and a headache are proof the vaccine is working. Also, after your cells know how to create spike proteins, your cells break down the mRNA and get rid of it. Oddly, the CDC made changes to its facts about Covid-19 mRNA vaccines in July 2022. Here is the CDC Fact Sheet from May 4th 2021:

---

Facts about COVID-19 mRNA Vaccines

They cannot give someone COVID-19.

- mRNA vaccines do not use the live virus that causes COVID-19.

They do not affect or interact with our DNA in any way.

- mRNA never enters the nucleus of the cell, which is where our DNA (genetic material) is kept.
- The cell breaks down and gets rid of the mRNA soon after it is finished using the instructions.

---

On July 23, 2022, notice how "The cell breaks down and gets rid of the mRNA soon after it is finished the instructions" was removed from the CDC Fact Sheet:

> ### Facts About mRNA COVID-19 Vaccines
>
> mRNA COVID-19 vaccines cannot give someone COVID-19 or other illnesses.
>
> - mRNA vaccines do not use any live virus.
> - mRNA vaccines cannot cause infection with the virus that causes COVID-19 or other viruses.
>
> They do not affect or interact with our DNA.
>
> - mRNA from these vaccines do not enter the nucleus of the cell where our DNA (genetic material) is located, so it cannot change or influence our genes.

Essentially, mRNA stays in a person's body and keeps instructing the cells to make spike proteins. It seems a person's body can become a spike protein creating factory for some time. That's a problem. Here are 4 doctors and a study out of Sweden which discuss the problem with mRNA and spike proteins in the body:

## 1- Dr. Byram Brindle, virologist, immunologist, vaccinologist, talks about spike proteins

Dr Brindle was demonized, harassed and cancel-cultured in the media for sounding the alarm about spike proteins in May of 2021. It seems he has been proven correct. From his September 18th 2022 article **Moderna's CMO Believes Spikes from the mRNA Vaccine Get to the Heart** we read:

*"The peer-reviewed scientific literature is also starting to confirm that the spike protein encoded by mRNA vaccines gets to unexpected and unwanted sites in the body, like the heart, where it causes myocarditis that is more severe and long-lasting than what the so-called narrative purports.*

*In short, likely mechanisms of COVID-19 vaccine-induced myocarditis include:*

1. *The mRNA vaccines get distributed to the heart where they program cells to manufacture and express the spike protein, thereby making the cells targets for spike-specific antibodies and T cells.*

2. *Some spike proteins may get into circulation and cause direct damage to cells in the heart when they bind to the ACE-2 receptor.*

*I found that speaking the truth about a connection between mRNA vaccines and myocarditis and opining on the possible mechanisms of action was generally not received well 1.5 years ago. I wonder if the naysayers will listen to the COVID-19 'vaccine' manufacturers as they now confirm this 1.5-year-old message."*

Dr. Brindle had sounded the alarm, but had been ignored. Why?

## 2- Dr Remnant discusses the problem with mRNA in a person's body

Dr Remnant describes himself on Substack as a "Rogue Doctor discovering health from perspectives that challenge the Medical-Industrial Orthodoxy". He wrote an article called **First Principles | The Problem with Gene-based Injections - Part 1.** (February 6, 2022) In it he had a major disagreement with the CDC claim that your body gets rid of mRNA months before the CDC dropped their claim.

(To better understand what Dr. Remnant is saying: LNP is the abbreviation for lipidnanoparticles, which are the capsules that carry mRNA to your cells. Recall that mRNA is the genetic material in the Pfizer and Moderna vaccines that uses your cells machinery to produce spike proteins.)

Dr Remnant said this about how mRNA vaccines affect the cells in your body:

*"Before your cells fused with LNPs they were healthy. After vaccination, the killer T-cells now view those healthy cells as infected and thus requiring destruction...This is the definition of an autoimmune response – a vaccinated person's immune system turns on its own healthy cells...*

*...the global population is being injected with a drug that can generate an autoimmune response against any cell in the body. Some people will develop more severe complications than others.*

*It is consistent with the observation that those who suffer* **the worst complications from the injection, tend to be young & healthy - AKA with healthy & robust immune systems.**

**Strong immune system → Strong autoimmune response."**

Are we seeing more autoimmune diseases since the mass vaccination campaign in 2021? A recent google search showed many results. I took a screen shot of two scientific articles published on the National Institute of Health's website.

https://www.ncbi.nlm.nih.gov › articles › PMC8979721

Autoimmune post-COVID vaccine syndromes - NCBI

by LJ Jara · Cited by 6 — Despite the **increasing** number of reports regarding **autoimmune** syndromes following **vaccination** against COVID-19, the incidence is very low, and the benefit...
Abstract · Vaccines, autoimmunity, and... · Post-COVID-19 vaccine... · Conclusion

https://pubmed.ncbi.nlm.nih.gov › ...

New-onset autoimmune phenomena post-COVID-19 vaccination

by Y Chen · Cited by 56 — Recently, new-onset **autoimmune** phenomena after COVID-19 **vaccination** have been reported increasingly (e.g. **immune** thrombotic thrombocytopenia,...

Note how the first article ("...the incidence is very low and the benefit...") seems to claim that the benefit of Covid vaccination outweighs the risks of an autoimmune disease. The second article says "Recently, now-onset autoimmune phenomenon after Covid-19 vaccination have been reported increasingly..."

It takes a lot of hubris to mandate that people take the risk of an autoimmune disease or any other health problem, which is exactly what has happened. It seems to me that government science agencies will never say anything directly negative about Covid vaccines.

**3- A study out of Sweden talks about mRNA and spike proteins**

On March 17th 2022 The **Scandinavian Journal of Immunology** published a letter to the editor which included comments on a study conducted by Pfizer for Japanese regulatory agencies, which wanted to make sure that the Pfizer vaccines were safe. In part the report reads (my underlining):

"*...a pharmacokinetic study performed by Pfizer for the Japanese regulatory agency shows that the LNPs (Lipid Nano Particles- the fatty capsules containing the mRNA) display an off-target distribution on rodents, accumulating in organs such as the spleen, liver, pituitary gland, thyroid, ovaries and in other tissues. ...*

*Another harmful source of toxicity has proven to be the spike protein itself. A study measured the longitudinal plasma samples collected from recipients of the mRNA-1273 Moderna vaccine. The study shows that considerable amounts of spike protein... can be detected in the blood plasma several days after the inoculation.*"

**If the lipid nano particles are accumulating in organs in rodents could that mean that they are accumulating in organs in people too?**

## 4- Dr. Peter McCullough talks about spike proteins

Dr. McCullough is a cardiologist with over 30 years of medical experience and was the former vice chief of internal medicine at Baylor University Medical Center located in Dallas, Texas. He is a leading expert on cardiovascular medicine and speaks widely about the heart-related risks that he believes can be attributed to mRNA vaccines, including myocarditis and adverse reactions in high endurance athletes. Dr McCullough is well-known for treating people in the early stages of a Covid infections. He is reported to have saved thousands of lives. He co-authored a paper found in the science journal Food and Chemical Toxicology in its June 2022 edition:

 Food and Chemical Toxicology

Volume 164, June 2022, 113008

Innate immune suppression by SARS-CoV-2 mRNA vaccinations: The role of G-quadruplexes, exosomes, and MicroRNAs

Stephanie Seneff [a], Greg Nigh [b], Anthony M. Kyriakopoulos [c], Peter A. McCullough [d]

The highlights of this article include:

*"mRNA vaccines promote sustained synthesis of the SARS-CoV-2 spike protein…"*

(What that means is that your body keeps making spike protein.)

*"The spike protein is neurotoxic, and it impairs DNA repair mechanisms"…*

The spike protein is Neurotoxin means that the spike protein is harmful to nerve tissue, which means spike protein can affect a person's nerves and brain. Impairs DNA repair mechanism is serious because DNA damage is a cause of cancer. Might we be seeing an increase in cancers now and into the future?

Again, who has the power to mandate that a person takes this risk?

**5- Dr. Ryan Cole, pathologist, talks about mRNA and spike proteins**

Dr. Ryan Cole is a pathologist and is the founder of Cole Diagnostics, an independent, full-service medical laboratory in Boise, Idaho. He is licensed in many states across the US and serves patients and clinicians across the country by providing diagnoses. In addition to being a pathologist, Dr. Cole specializes in immune health and early Covid treatments and has a treatment protocol for long Covid.

Dr. Cole is very concerned about spike proteins causing blood clots. He is seeing many very long blood clots, more than ever before in his career. (see blood clot image next page).

On his website, Dr. Cole doesn't write long scientific articles, but rather gives interviews in language that non-scientists and non-medical people can understand.

On June 4th 2022 Dr. Cole was on the news show **USA Watchdog**. The show was entitled **Global CV19 Vax Absolute Insanity – Dr. Ryan Cole**

Here are quotes from the show (my underlining):

*"I know there was a lot of coercion (to take Covid vaccines), which is very unfortunate because it's not what we do in medicine, yet, for whatever reason, we went into this mass psychosis societally…"*

---

*"...we are using a dangerous gene-based product without long term safety studies. A lot of people have received it. <u>We are seeing damage and autoimmune disease. We are seeing death from all causes at increased rates.</u>"*

*"This shot was a mistake. We rolled it out on humanity as an experiment. We were told it was approved, safe and effective, and they lied to humanity. The problem is it's a nuclear bomb platform. It's a Lipid Nanoparticle plus <u>a modified mRNA that you can't turn off</u>. It's a nuclear bomb, and we don't know the long-term safety and outcomes."*

Here is a picture of blood clots taken out of a deceased Covid vaccinated person:

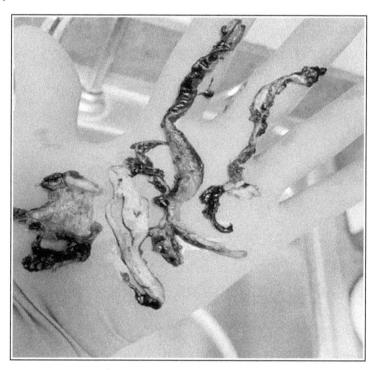

Tell me exactly why Covid vaccines that cause such blood clots should be required to attend many colleges and universities, to enlist or stay in the armed forces and to work at certain workplaces.

Do you think it is moral that vaccines proven to be this risky have been recommended by the CDC to be on the Children's Vaccination Schedule required to attend school?

If I had school age children, I would be opting out of public education and would not put them in any school that required Covid vaccinations.

**Is the truth a political decision or is there a truth?**

In the US, we now have state government leaders and attorney generals who have widely differing views on Covid vaccination. The Florida Health Department examined the cases of people who had suddenly died within 25 weeks of getting a Covid vaccine. Their analysis found that males age 18-39 had an increased risk of cardiac-related death and that people over the age of 65 had a 10% higher chance of a cardiac-related death within 28 days of mRNA vaccination. Florida Attorney General Dr. Joseph A Ladopo's tweet (below) which announced those findings was restricted (not shown) on Friday October 7 and then was reinstated on Sunday October 9. The truth won't stay hidden. That's a good thing.

Meanwhile, on the other side of the US, in Washington state, another Attorney General, Bob Ferguson, won't allow media members into his press conferences unless they show proof of being fully vaccinated and boosted. He doesn't provide evidence for his hard exclusion. I guess AG Ferguson hasn't been keeping up with the breakthrough deaths in the fully vaccinated (including those boosted) in his own state as highlighted in chapter 2 and hasn't accepted the fact that Covid vaccines don't prevent infection. I can understand screening people out of meetings who are sick, however asking for proof of vaccination status is going too far.

I'm embarrassed for AG Ferguson if he doesn't know basic facts about the vaccines not preventing transmission or infection.

In response to AG Ferguson's decision, Seattle journalist Jason Rantz wrote:

*"Ferguson, Democrat lawmakers, and Seattle media members see the vaccine as a status symbol. They think proving their status establishes them as some kind of pro-science hero in a sea of "dirty" anti-science Republicans. And it has the bonus, to them, of pushing out conservative media members who are either unvaccinated or refuse to give private medical information to a government agency to operate as a member of the free press. I fall into the latter camp, though in fairness, I don't often attend any press conferences."*

Has Covid vaccination become a status symbol, a way for people to virtue signal and self-identify as being a good person?

In the next chapter we will look at Covid vaccine mandates.

# 10... Covid Vaccine Mandates

*"Suddenly, those trusted institutions seemed to be acting in concert to generate fear, promote obedience, discourage critical thinking, and herd seven billion people to march to a single tune, culminating in mass public health experiments with a novel, shoddily tested and improperly licensed technology so risky that manufacturers refused to produce it unless every government on Earth shielded them from liability"* — Robert F. Kennedy Jr., The Real Anthony Fauci: Bill Gates, Big Pharma and the Global War on Democracy and Public Health

(Robert F Kennedy, Jr is the son of former Robert F. Kennedy, who was the US Attorney General from 1961-1964 and a US Senator from New York from 1965 until his assassination in 1968 while campaigning for the Democratic Party's presidential nomination. Robert F Kennedy, Jr. is an author, lawyer, and an advocate for the vaccine injured. He has researched the safety and efficacy of vaccines in general and Covid vaccines in particular.)

In this chapter my goal is to show you how vaccine mandates have negatively impacted a huge segment of the US population. I hope you will agree that mandating people take a Covid vaccine is wrong. We should have all stood up together against Covid vaccine mandates.

## Can't Force, but…
No one can physically force a person to get a Covid vaccine. However, as mentioned numerous times, a person can be barred from attending colleges or university, getting a job and serving in the military. Can you imagine the stress if you didn't want to take a Covid vaccine and your request for exemption was denied?

Many doors have been closed to the 33% of Americans who are unvaccinated. Many people were, for all intents and purposes, forced to get a Covid vaccine against their will. History won't remember the Covid era kindly. Millions of young people who aren't and won't take a Covid vaccine are unable to basically get their lives started or at least the lives they had wanted. It's wrong that we as a free people in the US are going along with this.

Thanks to the hard work of a member of the group No College Mandates, on July 13th 2022 a google doc was created with a list of colleges and universities nationwide and their vaccine requirements. Here is a screen shot of a list of Washington state universities and their Covid vaccination requirements:

| | | City | State | Student Mandate | | Last checked |
|---|---|---|---|---|---|---|
| | | | | Vax | Booster | |
| 1020 | Central Washington University | Ellensburg | WA | yes | no | 8/19/22 |
| 1021 | Eastern Washington University | Cheney | WA | yes | no | 8/19/22 |
| 1022 | Evergreen State College | Olympia | WA | yes | no | 8/19/22 |
| 1023 | Gonzaga University | Spokane | WA | yes | no | 8/19/22 |
| 1024 | Northwest University | Kirkland | WA | yes | no | 8/19/22 |
| 1025 | Pacific Lutheran University | Tacoma | WA | yes | yes | 8/19/22 |
| 1026 | Puget Sound, University of the | Tacoma | WA | yes | yes | 8/19/22 |
| 1027 | Saint Martin's University | Lacey | WA | yes | no | 8/19/22 |
| 1028 | Seattle Pacific University | Seattle | WA | yes | no | 8/19/22 |
| 1029 | Seattle University | Seattle | WA | yes | yes | 8/19/22 |
| 1030 | Walla Walla University | College Place | WA | yes | no | 8/19/22 |
| 1031 | Washington State University | Pullman | WA | yes | no | 8/19/22 |
| 1032 | Washington, Univ of (Tacoma) | Tacoma | WA | yes | no | 8/19/22 |
| 1033 | Washington, University of    UW | Seattle | WA | yes | no | 8/19/22 |
| 1034 | Washington, University of (Bothell) | Bothell | WA | yes | no | 8/19/22 |
| 1035 | Western Washington Univ | Bellingham | WA | yes | no | 8/19/22 |
| 1036 | Whitman College | Walla Walla | WA | yes | yes | 8/19/22 |
| 1037 | Whitworth University | Spokane | WA | yes | no | 8/19/22 |

Note that 4 of the 18 universities require boosters. (The URL to this google doc is in the Appendix.)

Despite being institutes of higher education, many of the college and university board of trustees, administrators, faculty and staff don't seem to have done much research on Covid vaccine efficacy or risks or haven't thought much about possible long-term effects. They haven't realized the dangers in allowing powerful forces to mandate pharmaceuticals. What might those forces mandate next? Likely a great many individuals in higher education do disagree with the Covid vaccine mandates, but they are afraid of saying anything due to peer pressure and the fear of being cancel-cultured. Also, big companies like Google, Facebook, Netflix, and Lyft have Covid vaccine mandates in place. I recently heard that AT&T even requires full vaccination of their at home workers.

In November 2021, President Biden announced a new mandatory vaccination program for all US businesses with 100 or more employees. He announced that all employees (though not fully online employees) were mandated to take Covid vaccines or do weekly testing to prove they did not have a Covid infection. He was going to give OSHA authority to supervise this program.

Thankfully, the US Supreme Court stopped the mandatory vaccination program in January 2022. They said it exceeding OSHA's authority. It was a 6-3 vote.

Sadly, many, if not most, US children could be mandated to take Covid vaccines to attend public school. On October 20th 2022, the CDC's vaccine advisory committee voted unanimously (15-0) to add Covid vaccines to the childhood vaccination schedule. The new vaccination schedule will be rolled out in February 2023. Thankfully, vaccine mandates are decided at the state and local levels; however, it is likely most blue states will go along with the CDC vaccine advisory committee's decision. Commenting on the 15-0 vote, Robert F. Kennedy Jr, chairman of the board and chief legal counsel for Children's Health Defense, said:

*"This reckless action is final proof of the cynicism, corruption and capture of a once exemplary public health agency. ACIP (Advisory Committee on Immunization Practices) members have again demonstrated that fealty to their pharma overlords eclipses any residual concerns they may harbor for child welfare or public health.*

*"This is an act of child abuse on a massive scale."*

I imagine that a lot of parents will be searching for alternatives to public education or otherwise move to a state not requiring childhood Covid vaccination. I applaud them.

**The push back against vaccine mandates**
The Screen Actors Guild and the American Federation of Television and Radio Artists have a union known by its abbreviations: SAG-AFTRA. They represent approximately 160,000 actors, announcers, broadcast journalists, dancers, DJs, news writers, news editors, etc. SAG-AFTRA is affiliated with the AFL-CIO and mandates Covid vaccination for its members. The president of the SAG-AFTRA is actress Fran Drescher, famous for her role as Fran Fine in the television sitcom The Nanny. Drescher herself is vaccinated but wishes to see the Covid vaccine mandate that SAG-AFTRA approved be repealed in September 2022 when it is up for review.

In the August 11th 2022 article **President Fran Drescher Calls For Review Of Hollywood's Covid Vaccination Mandate,** Drescher said:

*"…. with thousands of unvaccinated members still unable to work, all new information begs review and consideration before deciding our position on the next RTWA (Return to work agreement). All I ask is we educate ourselves with the newest science and make an informed decision because members' livelihoods hang in the balance."*

I applaud Fran Dresher's clear thinking.

The NBA also announced that they will not require vaccination for its players in the 2022-2023 season.

As mentioned, 1,000's of colleges and universities nationwide have Covid vaccination mandates.

Yet some are slowly being repealed by the school's governing boards.  For example, vaccine mandates were lifted at the three Ventura County community colleges in California.  On August 20th 2022 in the article **Days before classes start, vaccine mandate lifted at Ventura County community colleges**, we read:

*"Students at Ventura County's three community colleges no longer need COVID-19 vaccines to enroll in on-campus classes after board trustees voted unanimously Tuesday night to lift the requirement...*

*"We are in a very different place than we were two years ago, a very different place than we were a year ago," Rick MacLennan, the district's new chancellor, said during the meeting. "Public policy is generally shifting away from institutional mandates to individual responsibility…. Students were split on the vaccine mandate, with 60% in favor and 40% opposed in a July survey conducted by the district. Of those opposed to the vaccine mandate, 41% said they would not enroll in classes if the requirement remained. Just 8% of students in favor said they would unenroll if the mandate was lifted."*

Thank goodness.


**What's happening to unvaccinated college-age people?**
In Washington state far fewer students have been going to college and university since Covid vaccines have been mandated. Thousands of college students have decided the benefit of an education was not worth the risk of destroying their health.

I was contacted by one graduate student at Evergreen State College to talk about his unvaccinated status, vaccine exemptions and what is going on at his college. One thing he shared was that he can't believe how everyone is so easily going along with the Covid vaccine mandates and that no one is talking about any aspect of the Covid response, as if Covid is a taboo topic.

The article **Enrollment plummets at Washington Colleges**... in the Seattle Times (April 24th 2022) discusses the dramatic decrease in college enrollment in Washington:

*"Community and technical colleges experienced a combined 24% drop between fall 2019 and fall 2021. Public four-year institutions saw a collective drop in undergraduates of nearly 7% during that time period, with some schools' losses double or even triple that. Roughly 60,000 fewer students, in all, enrolled."*

My guess is that the students didn't want to get vaccinated. I wouldn't have taken a Covid vaccine to enter college either if I were in their shoes.

The college vaccination mandate is very sad to me. I was a college professor for nearly 30 years, so I know how much people can benefit from a college education. They learn a wide curriculum of knowledge and how to analyze information. They learn how to write, which is not a simple feat. They learn how to get along with people who are unlike themselves. They learn job skills. A college degree opens the door to a bigger world and leads to opportunities.

I've talked to many unvaccinated young people who want to attend college or graduate school. Instead, their lives are at a standstill. Instead of achieving their dreams, they are working at jobs that don't require vaccination and many are struggling with mental health issues.

## Mandating State Workers Get Boosters

On July 1st 2022 Washington state Governor Jay Inslee mandated that all state agency employees be fully boosted by July 1, 2023. On the news site My Northwest we saw the following headline:

**Gov. Inslee permanently mandates COVID-19 vaccines for WA agency employees**

The governor declared:

*"Impacted employees (62,000 state agency employees) must be "up to date" on their COVID vaccine series, including additional booster doses recommended by the Center for Disease Control by July 1, 2023."*

What was his reasoning? His proclamation reads:

*""COVID-19 vaccines are effective in reducing infection and serious disease, and widespread vaccination is the primary means we have as a state to protect everyone, including persons who cannot be vaccinated for medical reasons, immunocompromised individuals, and vulnerable persons including persons in health care facilities, long-term care facilities and other congregate care facilities from COVID-19 infections..."*

(I wonder how Governor Inslee has to say in response to the nearly 3,000 Covid related deaths in fully vaccinated people through From January 2021- September 2022 in WA state.)

When I read Inslee's proclamation, I predicted that many of those 62,000 state agency employees would refuse Covid booster shots and would either retire early or change jobs, like many teachers and health workers have done since vaccine mandates went into effect. Many state agency employees would take booster(s) begrudgingly.

One reason I wrote this book is to reason with the Covid vaccine mandaters, people who favor Covid vaccine mandates. I have confidence that in due time they will change their minds and all Covid vaccine mandates will be repealed.

Thankfully, due to the latest change in CDC Covid guidelines, Governor Inslee changed his mind about forcing all state agency employees to be up-to-date on their boosters. Now state employees won't be forced to be boosted to keep their jobs. Instead they will be incentivized to take the boosters. Soon after his July 1, 2022 mandate, Governor Inslee declared:

*"I direct [the Office of Financial Management] to pursue options to incentivize all state executive and small cabinet agency employees to remain fully vaccinated with the most up-to-date vaccination, including any additional doses or boosters, as recommended by the CDC."*

If people don't want a Covid vaccine or a Covid booster, giving them $1,000 or even $10,000 won't change their mind.

To give one more example of the push against vaccine mandates, on September 24th, 2021 many pairs of shoes and 59 notes were left outside the Spokane Public Schools building in downtown Spokane, the biggest city in eastern Washington state. These public school employees were asking for a halt to the Covid vaccine mandate.

The notes they left next to or under the shoes often included the workers' years of service, why they were being fired and why they support medical freedom.

Words escape me.

**Shoes, notes left outside Spokane Public Schools building in protest of state vaccine mandate**
(Sept. 24, 2021 from the Spokesman-Review)

The people in power need to listen to and address the concerns being raised by so many people. What does it mean to live in the US if they don't?

Why are so many people, who have done little to no independent research outside of their media bubble, so smug, so self-righteous and so dismissive of information that they simply do not know?

Why do they want us all vaccinated? To me, that is the question.

Thankfully, there are challenges to vaccine mandates taking place nationwide. A group of 16 NY city sanitation workers who lost their jobs due to refusing Covid vaccination won their case in court against the city of NY.

# New York City appeals judge's ruling that could reinstate fired unvaccinated employees

Tuesday, October 25, 2022 2:37PM

Staten Island Supreme Court Justice Ralph Porzio stated in his ruling:

*"Being vaccinated does not prevent an individual from contracting or transmitting Covid-19"...and that "If it was about public safety and health, no one would be exempt."*

The ruling reinstates the workers to their jobs with back pay. However, NYC is appealing because it wants all public employees to be vaccinated, and until that court rules, the vaccine mandate will remain in effect.

In a separate earlier development, the entire NYC Board of Health voted to repeal the vaccine mandate for private employees, which was announced by NY Mayor Eric Adams on September 20th 2022.

Talk about a battle. Which side do you think will ultimately prevail?

The next chapter is a letter from a second year medical student and his thoughts and questions about the vaccine mandate at his university.

---

# 11... A Letter from a Second Year Medical Student

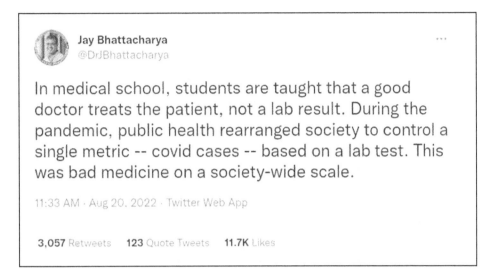

Dr. Jay Bhattacharya (1968-) is a professor of Medicine at Stanford University. He has vocally opposed masking, lockdowns and Covid vaccines. He co-authored the Great Barrington Declaration which a set of guidelines in how we should have (in my opinion also) responded to the Covid virus by letting the virus spread in lower-risk groups with the aim of herd immunity, and have "focused protection" of those at the highest risk of dying from a Covid infection.

In this chapter my goal is to show you a letter written by a medical student who was in medical school at the start of the Covid outbreak. I hope you will see how many very educated people questioned the Covid mandates and Covid vaccines and the reasons they had.

I came across this letter on Dr. Vinay Prasad's Substack page: **Medical School During COVID-19: A Student's Thoughts.** It was written by a second year medical student who wanted to shares his perceptions of attending medical school during Covid.

**By Anonymous, East Coast Medical Student**

I just finished my first year of medical school! Many wonderful things happened, and I hope to share these some day, but today I want to describe my thoughts on COVID-19, and how my university's policies affected my education. I was a premed student when the virus hit, and I didn't know how scared to be.

Like many, I followed the pandemic from the beginning. I watched as President Trump described the dangers of the novel virus. I'll admit, I feared what was to come. In the beginning, we didn't know what the virus was capable of and weren't getting reassurance from mainstream media. If anything, they made things worse.

Many medical doctors and PhD scientists began speaking on TV claiming to be 'experts' regarding SARS-CoV-2. Many of their messages weren't data driven, and unfortunately, were fear driven. No wonder the world went crazy. I remember thinking then, and still to this day, how can these individuals be experts? This is a novel virus, and the world has little to no experience dealing with a pandemic of this magnitude, so how can someone be an expert in something that has never existed?

During the first few weeks of the pandemic (March 2020), we were talking about interventions that had never been attempted in all of human history – shutting down school, borders, and society itself – even if these 'experts' knew everything possible about corona virus transmission, how could they know which of these interventions, if any, were justified? Which would have unintended consequences?

The real experts were those who were silent, spending their time critically evaluating all the data to derive objective conclusions decoupled from their political ideology – only speaking when having something relevant and important to say.

When watching an April 3rd, 2020 YouTube video by Prof. John Ioannidis, I felt for the first time that I was being spoken to honestly. He simply described that there was uncertainty about the severity of COVID-19 and that we currently were lacking reliable data. He then explained that fatality rates from a Carnival Cruise outbreak were much lower and likely more accurate than estimates by the WHO (3.4% CFR). His message was objective, calming, and in stark contrast with messages from the mainstream media.

I often wonder how the public's perception of the pandemic would have differed if the CDC and mainstream media would have adopted a similar message to Dr. Ioannidis.

Unfortunately, one of Professor Ioannidis' videos was removed in the early days of the pandemic because of the claim – that COVID-19 might have an IFR in the same ballpark as the worst seasonal influenza. But how could this claim be wrong? Who decides how big a ballpark is? I found the censorship surreal.

As time passed, it seemed our response to the virus moved further and further away from the data, and, at least from my perspective, further away from the truth and common sense.

**I get accepted to medical school, conditional on vaccination**

Fast forward to Spring 2021. I was fortunate and got my medical school acceptance letter early, so thankfully I wasn't one of those students who struggled with the anxiety of potentially not being admitted.

Nonetheless, my worries found me as I learned that my university would be mandating the COVID-19 vaccine for students. I wasn't ready to take the COVID-19 vaccine. Plain and simple, I wanted to know more about the efficacy in my age group, and I hoped to see robust safety data before making this decision.

In my mind, mandatory vaccines are only justified if we know that the adverse event risk to the recipient is trivial, that vaccination protects the health of others, and that natural infection is insufficient to do so. Other vaccines are mandatory for medical school, but students can opt-out by showing evidence of pre-existing antibodies. However, for COVID-19 there was no alternative to vaccination even if an individual had detectable antibody levels.

I thought there must be a reason for this – But, I am still waiting! Vaccinated and naturally infected individuals both produce antibodies against the spike protein – those infected naturally actually have additional antibodies specific to other motifs on the virus.

Moreover, the risk of bad outcomes from reinfection appears lower in those with natural immunity than those merely vaccinated. Finally, escape variants have rendered both natural immunity and vaccination defenseless against reinfection. My question remains: why is natural immunity not considered a vaccine equivalent? It surely is.

Not only my university, but all mainstream public health agencies have consistently discredited any immunity gained from natural infection. Of all the blunders public health has committed over the pandemic, this one may only be rivaled by school closures and will lead to years of distrust.

Countless studies have now been published supporting what many of us already knew – immunity post infection is robust, long lasting, and durable. Yet, to this day, the US. government and CDC are hesitant to acknowledge immunity gained from infection...

My university prides itself on practicing and teaching evidence based medicine, yet the COVID-19 policies they have implemented are vastly discordant with the evidence base. I'm afraid my university values its image over pursuing sensible, data driven guidelines. Despite having intelligent physicians and public health leaders making decisions, it seems they would rather fit in with the crowd (follow suit with other universities) than use their judgment to make and adapt policy. I don't blame them for 'following the leader' as it is quite challenging to be the one pushing against the grain. However, I am disappointed to be at an institution that (through the lens of COVID-19 policy) appears to discredit the truth and lack urgency in finding it.

**How has COVID affected my medical education?**

In all honesty, I don't believe COVID has impacted the quality of my medical education. Despite vaccine/booster/mask mandates, routine asymptomatic testing, random breaks from in-person learning, and a constant reminder that COVID is real and dangerous, I don't feel cheated out of critical learning experiences. At the same time, I will admit, I don't know what things could have been like had we had sensible policies.

Although the policies/restrictions were burdensome, I learned to live with them. Preparing to be a competent doctor who provides the best possible care to patients is far more important than letting ill-advised policies affect my education. I suppose the policies gave me a chance to show my resiliency.

Finally, the pandemic will likely remain a guiding principle throughout my life – even if my university still has not heeded the lessons. This experience has convinced me that "in God we trust, but everyone else must bring [honest] data". I am now much more critical of what I read and arrive at conclusions that are derived from my thoughts rather than parroting what others say.

I wish there were easier ways to have been taught this lesson, but I am grateful to have learned it and know it will serve me and my patients well. Thank you for reading my experience."

This medical student has had years of science classes, questions the vaccines and wonders about the legitimacy of the vaccine mandates. He thinks deeply about health. I would like him to be my doctor someday.

Why are so many government and public health people acting so confident and sure in their response to Covid? Why don't they talk to the sizable number of people who disagree with them? Why their smug dismissal of our concerns and facts?

In the next chapter we will look at the risk of dying in different age groups relative to their population.

# 12... Risk of dying from all causes vs the chance of a death involving Covid

*"It's only when we truly know and understand that we have a limited time on earth – and that we have no way of knowing when our time is up – that we will begin to live each day to the fullest, as if it was the only one we had"*

– Elizabeth Kubler-Ross (1926-2004) was a psychiatrist who wrote the internationally best-selling book **On Death and Dying** in which she introduced her theory of the 5 stages of dying. She was named by Time magazine as one of the hundred most important thinkers in the 20th century.

In this chapter my goal is to show you the chance a person had in different age groups of dying from any cause and involving Covid based on the population of each age group. I hope that you will see that Covid is not a major risk to young people and agree that the mandating of an experimental and risky vaccine that doesn't even work as promised is unjust and immoral.

Fewer than **8,000** people under the age of 30 had a Covid-related death from **March 2020-August 28th 2022** out of a total population of roughly **120 million**. Yet, colleges and universities, many workplaces and the US military mandate that students, workers and military members get vaccinated. Why?

I ask why because there were **249** deaths reported to VAERS associated with the Covid vaccine in the 0-30 year old population up to September 23rd 2022. Here are the first two reports of deaths on OpenVAERS:

Total number of reports: 246                                   ● Died  ● Permanently Disabled  ● Life Threatening

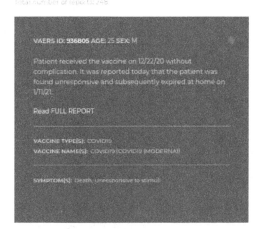

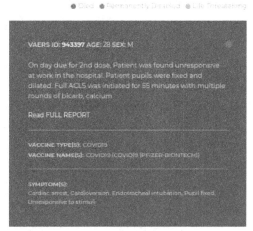

Because they are hard to read, I'll summarize each report. The first report is a 25 year old male who received a Covid vaccine on 12/22/20 and was found at home dead on 1/11/21. The second report is a 29 year old male who, on the day he was due in for his second dose, was found dead at the hospital where he worked. Of course, those deaths could have occurred anyway without Covid vaccination; however they were reported to VAERS as associated with Covid vaccines. Vaccine mandates are forcing people to assume risk of death if they take the Covid vaccine. Again, is that moral?

When you look at the total population of 0-17 year olds and 18-29 year olds, their chance of having a death involving Covid is close to zero. Their chance of dying from anything else isn't much higher.

Media exaggerated the risk of Covid related death. Their efforts to make people fear dying from Covid seem to have succeeded.

It may have been because of the perceptions of risk that students, soldiers and some employees have been mandated to take Covid vaccines. Most of those who do the mandating probably believe that Covid vaccines stop infection, transmission, death and that they are safe.

However, once the mandaters realize they have been lied to about the safety and efficacy of Covid vaccines, they will have to change their policies (or remain immoral)- the sooner the better.

My hope in writing this chapter is to assure people that the risk of having a Covid-related death is low, and very slight in younger populations. I really don't understand the reasoning behind Covid vaccine mandates except to sell vaccines.

**Population**

To ascertain the risk of dying from any cause or from a Covid-related cause, we need to know the total population of a person's age group. If we know the total population of an age group and the number of people who died in in that age group in a year, we can do simple math and know the risk a person has of dying. Knowing the true risk of death helps us combat the fearful messaging and the associated anxiety that we experience.

Let's start with the population of different age groups in the US:

## US Population (2020)

| Age group | Approximate population |
|-----------|------------------------|
| 0-17      | 71.3 million           |
| 18-29     | 48.8 million           |
| 30-39     | 44.7 million           |
| 40-49     | 40.3 million           |
| 50-64     | 62.8 million           |
| 65-74     | 32.5 million           |
| 75-84     | 16.5 million           |
| 85+       | 6.7 million            |

This chart shows the total population of each age group and the total number of deaths from all causes (including Covid) – according to the CDC- in 2020, 2021 and 2022 (through September 3rd):

**US- Total Deaths from All Causes**

| Age group | Approximate population | Total Deaths from all causes 2020 | Total Deaths from all causes 2021 | Total Deaths from all causes 2022 (to Sept 3rd) |
|---|---|---|---|---|
| 0-17 | 71.3 million | 34,204 | 35,789 | 21,392 |
| 18-29 | 48.8 million | 63,520 | 68,114 | 37,260 |
| 30-39 | 44.7 million | 89,319 | 104,177 | 57,840 |
| 40-49 | 40.3 million | 133,464 | 155,548 | 84,074 |
| 50-64 | 62.8 million | 557,214 | 610,293 | 336,580 |
| 65-74 | 32.5 million | 675,490 | 725,850 | 426,051 |
| 75-84 | 16.5 million | 823,038 | 830,710 | 523,815 |
| 85+ | 6.7 million | 1,013,340 | 941,309 | 593,736 |

It is interesting to see how many millions of Americans are in each age group. Compare the number of 85+ years olds to the number of 0-17 year olds in the US. There are only about **6.7** million 85+ year olds while there are **71.3** million people in the 0-17 year age group.

Every age group (besides 85+) saw a substantial increase in the number of deaths from any cause from 2020 to 2021. It will be interesting to see how many deaths occur by the end of 2022. So far, the number of deaths from all causes looks on track to being lower than in 2020.

Looking at the 65-74 year old age group, The population is **32.5** million and **about 81%** of people in that age group were fully vaccinated by June 24th 2021. Yet, there were an additional **50,360** deaths in that age group in 2021. It is very clear that the chance of dying in a given year increases as we age. For example, there are **71.3 million** children (0-17) in the US and from January to September 3, 2022 there were **21,392** deaths from any cause.

Compare that number to the number of 85+ year old people who died. There is a total of **6.7 million** elderly people in the US and from January to September 3ʳᵈ 2022 there were **593,736** deaths from any cause. Let's look at the percentage of people who died in each age group per year:

**Population and percentage of people who died in each age group per year <u>of any cause</u>**

| Age group | Approximate population | % who died 2020 | % who died 2021 | % who died 2022 (to Sept 3rd) |
|---|---|---|---|---|
| 0-17 | 71.3 million | 0.048% | 0.050% | 0.030% |
| 18-29 | 48.8 million | 0.13% | 0.14% | 0.076% |
| 30-39 | 44.7 million | 0.2% | 0.23% | 0.13% |
| 40-49 | 40.3 million | 0.33% | 0.39% | 0.21% |
| 50-64 | 62.8 million | 0.89% | 0.97% | 0.54% |
| 65-74 | 32.5 million | 2.08% | 2.23% | 1.31% |
| 75-84 | 16.5 million | 4.99% | 5.35% | 3.17% |
| 85+ | 6.7 million | 15.12% | 14.05% | 8.86% |

Let's remember that these aren't the percentage of people who died from a Covid infection. Rather, the percentages represent the number of people who died <u>from any cause</u>. Notice again how a greater percentage of people died in 2021 than in 2020 in all age groups except for the 85+ group. This is despite the majority of people over the age of 25 being fully vaccinated by June 2021.

Finally, notice how the chance of dying starting with the 40-49 year old age group more than doubles as a person leaves one age group and enters another. For example, in 2020 in the 50-64 age group **0.89%** died while in the next age group (65-74) **2.08%** died.

**Fear leads us**

The endless emotional portrayal of Covid hospitalization and death in 2020 and 2021 caused a lot of anxiety and palpable fear in the US population. Taking a Covid vaccine eased many people's anxiety. And then some of the people who got vaccinated got angry when they saw people refuse Covid vaccines. Here are two tweets among many that were going around in 2021:

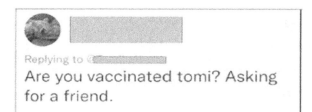

Replying to

Are you vaccinated tomi? Asking for a friend.

The unvaccinated shouldnt be allowed to benefit off the herd immunity the vaccinated are trying to reach.

Any unvaccinated should forego any medical aide when they get sick.

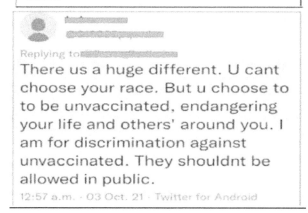

Replying to

There us a huge different. U cant choose your race. But u choose to to be unvaccinated, endangering your life and others' around you. I am for discrimination against unvaccinated. They shouldnt be allowed in public.

12:57 a.m. · 03 Oct. 21 · Twitter for Android

The system had created the fear and anxiety, provided a solution, and created an enemy, the people who stood outside of the herd. It has really been something to see and to experience as an unvaccinated person.

In fact, according to the results of a Heartland Institute and Rasmussen Report survey, the unvaccinated were still the enemy in many people's mind even in 2022. From the January 13<sup>th</sup> 2022 article **COVID-19: Democratic Voters Support Harsh Measures Against Unvaccinated we read:**

"Fifty-nine percent (59%) of Democratic voters would favor a government policy requiring that citizens remain confined to their homes at all times, except for emergencies, if they refuse to get a COVID-19 vaccine. Such a proposal is opposed by 61% of all likely voters, including 79% of Republicans and 71% of unaffiliated voters.

– Nearly half (48%) of Democratic voters think federal and state governments should be able to fine or imprison individuals who publicly question the efficacy of the existing COVID-19 vaccines on social media, television, radio, or in online or digital publications. Only 27% of all voters – including just 14% of Republicans and 18% of unaffiliated voters – favor criminal punishment of vaccine critics.

– Forty-five percent (45%) of Democrats would favor governments requiring citizens to temporarily live in designated facilities or locations if they refuse to get a COVID-19 vaccine."

No wonder so many people have assumed I'm a Republican.

The bottom line is that a great many people in the US have been successfully propagandized due to the efforts of players like the Gates Foundation and the World Economic Forum. As an unvaccinated person it's a little frightening to know that a great many people mistakenly hold these views.

After reading this report, I would be hard pressed to vote for any Democrat.

The fear that we might die or cause someone else to die conditioned many people to follow US leadership and media without question. Were we told the whole truth about Covid vaccines, like how Covid vaccines come with risks, how the vast majority of people who get a Covid infection don't die, and how Covid vaccines don't stop transmission, or infection and won't lead us to herd immunity?

**Deaths involving Covid vs deaths from other causes: 2020- 2022**
Let's look at deaths in different age groups in the entire time frame Jan. 1 2020 – August 28th 2022 to find the number of people who died from any cause and how many people had a death involving Covid. I want to get an idea of the ratio between deaths involving Covid and deaths from any other cause since the start of the Covid era. Here is a screen shot from the CDC showing the total number of deaths from any cause and the total number of deaths related to Covid since January 2020  (retrieved on August 28th 2022):

| | | | Deaths Involving Covid | Total Deaths All Causes |
|---|---|---|---|---|
| 2020-2022 | All Sexes | 0-17 years | 1,241 | 90,515 |
| 2020-2022 | All Sexes | 18-29 years | 6,522 | 167,368 |
| 2020-2022 | All Sexes | 30-39 years | 18,739 | 249,126 |
| 2020-2022 | All Sexes | 40-49 years | 44,082 | 370,326 |
| 2020-2022 | All Sexes | 50-64 years | 192,200 | 1,493,895 |
| 2020-2022 | All Sexes | 65-74 years | 237,039 | 1,815,256 |
| 2020-2022 | All Sexes | 75-84 years | 268,509 | 2,161,989 |
| 2020-2022 | All Sexes | 85 years and over | 270,467 | 2,531,119 |

Remember, we are looking at the entire time period of 2 years and 8 months. I copied the numbers to create this chart:

## US Deaths  (Jan 2020-August 28$^{th}$ 2022)

| Age group | Population | Total Deaths 2020-2022 | % who died from any cause 2020-2022 | Total Deaths involving Covid 2020-2022 | %deaths not involving Covid 2020-2022 | %deaths involving Covid 2020-2022 |
|---|---|---|---|---|---|---|
| 0-17 | 71.3 million | 90,515 | 0.13% | 1,241 | 98.63% | 1.37% |
| 18-29 | 48.8 million | 167,368 | 0.34% | 6,522 | 96.11% | 3.89% |
| 30-39 | 44.7 million | 249,126 | 0.56% | 18,739 | 92.5% | 7.5% |
| 40-49 | 40.3 million | 370,326 | 0.92% | 44,082 | 88.1% | 11.9% |
| 50-64 | 62.8 million | 1,493,895 | 2.37% | 192,200 | 87.1% | 12.9% |
| 65-74 | 32.5 million | 1,815,256 | 5.59% | 237,039 | 86.9% | 13.1% |
| 75-84 | 16.5 million | 2,161,989 | 13.1% | 268,509 | 87.6% | 12.4% |
| 85+ | 6.7 million | 2,531,119 | 37.8% | 270,467 | 89.4% | 10.6% |

Notice the number of Covid related deaths in each age group in relation to the group's population. Also, recall that when people die from any cause and test positive for Covid, the death certificate can say *Covid* as a cause. Look at my age group: 50-64. From 2020-August 2022, 0.92% (less than 1 person out of 100) died from anything- over a 2 ½ year period. Of those who died, 87% died from causes other than Covid.

Over this 2 ½ + year span, if we compare the percentage of deaths involving Covid to the percentage of deaths from other causes in the different age groups, we can see a few interesting things:

The older a person is the greater chance he or she has of a death related to Covid. Compare the **1,241** Covid-related deaths in the age group 0-17 (March 2020-August 2022) to the **192,200** deaths in the age group 50-64. And the 0-17 year old age group has about 8 million more people.

Young people are at virtually no risk of dying a Covid related death or any death when you keep in mind their entire population. Young people have always died, but we likely hadn't thought too much about it before Covid. Looking at the 0-17 age group, note that 0.13% of them died from anything over that 2 ½+ year period. Of those who died, 98.6% died from causes other than Covid.

My 30 year old son has lost four of his high school classmates: two from drug overdoses, one from gang violence and one from cancer. Those deaths were very sad and impacted him greatly, as death impacts us all. He hasn't had any friends die from a Covid infection.

I wonder how many healthy people with no underlying health problems, had a death involving Covid. It seems there are far greater chances of dying from drugs, depression, cancers and accidents.

Can you justify why Covid vaccines should be mandated?

In the next chapter we will look at excess mortality. There have been a lot of unexpected deaths in the US, especially in the working age population.

# 13... Excess Mortality

*"One reason most people never stop thinking is that mental frenzy keeps us from having to see the upsetting aspects of our lives. If I'm constantly brooding about my children or career, I won't notice that I'm lonely. If I grapple continuously with logistical problems, I can avoid contemplating little issues like, say, my own mortality."*

Martha Beck (1962-) is an American author, life coach, and speaker who helps individuals and groups achieve success. She has three degrees, a BA, MA and PhD from Harvard University.

In this chapter my goal to talk about excess mortality, the HUGE increase in deaths than from the number of deaths that had been expected in most age groups in the US in 2020, 2021 and 2022. The majority of these deaths can't be attributed to Covid. I hope that you will become curious about why so many people have been dying.

The website US Mortality keeps track of the number of deaths in the US. Here is why US Mortality say that it's important to keep track of mortality:

"Mortality is a basic indicator of health….With the emergence of new diseases or threats of epidemics (e.g. pandemic influenza, SARS), decision makers will need such data to estimate the severity of the problem and inform any initiatives to be put in place as part of an effective public health response... Mortality monitoring should be ongoing to detect when and where excess mortality occurs."

-US Mortality -in the *About Us* section of their website (All charts in this chapter were retrieved on August 17th 2022 from USMortality.)

**Excess Mortality**

Excess mortality means that more people die in a given time frame than were expected to die. Life insurance companies and government agencies regularly make predictions on how many people will die in a given year, so that they can more effectively make financial decisions. For example, in the case of the Social Security Administration, if fewer people are predicted to die, they will plan to spend less money. In the case of life insurance companies, if more people die than expected, it means less profit for the life insurance companies because more money is paid out in death benefits than taken in through insurance premiums.

The All-Cause Excess Mortality chart <u>for the entire US population</u> (below) shows us how many people died compared to the baseline (meaning zero excess deaths), The **band** indicates the normal range of deaths expected. The **dash line** indicates a substantial increase in deaths. The **dark line** is the number of people who were reported to have died. (I put in the vertical lines to indicate the years.)

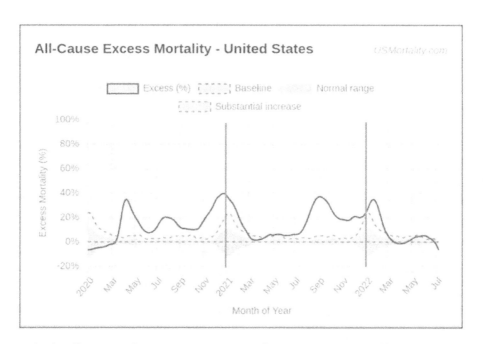

The Y axis indicates the percentage of excess mortality.

In roughly April 2020 the excess mortality rate was 38% (38% more than what had been expected). The most excess deaths occurred in December 2020 at 40% and in September 2021 at near 40%. In January 2022 the excess mortality rate was 35%. Since April 2022 the number of deaths are in the expected or less than expected range.

**Cumulative Excess Mortality – US all ages**

In this chart from USMortality we see the cumulative record of deaths in 2020, 2021 and 2022, a running total of excess deaths:

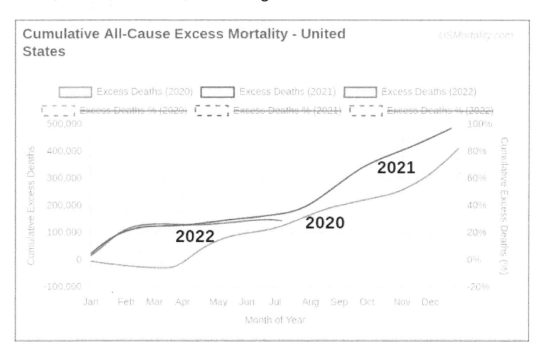

I wrote in the years under the lines. The 2022 line goes through the beginning part of July.

USMortality gives us the number of deaths that had been expected for 2020, 2021 and 2022 and the number of deaths that were reported. Subtracting the expected deaths from the reported deaths, we get the number of excess deaths. (I copied USMortality's words here. I bolded the % increase in deaths.)

**2020**: United States reported 3,440,580 deaths of all ages for the year 2020. Expected deaths were 3,028,959. That is an increase of 411,621 deaths **(+13.6%)**.

**2021:** United States reported 3,457,632 deaths of all ages for the year 2021. Expected deaths were 2,971,452. That is an increase of 486,180 deaths **(+16.4%)**.

**2022:** To date, for the year 2022, United States reported 1,700,062 deaths of all ages. Expected deaths thus far, were 1,570,883. That is an increase of 129,179 deaths **(+8.2%)**."

Let's see what those numbers look like in a chart:

## US Deaths- All Ages

| Year | Deaths expected | Deaths reported | Excess deaths | Percent increase |
|------|-----------------|-----------------|---------------|------------------|
| 2020 | 3,028,959 | 3,440,580 | 411,621 | +13.6% |
| 2021 | 2,971,452 | 3,457,632 | 486,180 | +16.4% |
| 2022 (July) | 1,570,883 | 1,700,062 | 129,179 | +8.2% |

Adding the three years of excess deaths together, over a million more people have died than expected since January 2020.

Note the percentage increase in death each year. A 10% rise in death is almost unheard of according to insurance companies. Again, in 2020 there was a **+13.6%** increase, in 2021 there was a **16.4%** increase and in 2022 (Jan-July) there was an **8.2%** increase. It turns out that Insurance companies are paying out a record amount of money in non-Covid related death claims, which we will look at in detail soon.

What were the differences between the earlier years (2015-2019) and 2020, 2021 and 2022 that caused so many excess deaths?

The differences I can think of are the Covid virus, the Covid mandates, which did result in deaths of despair and putting off medical treatments which led to death, and the introduction of the Covid vaccine in 2021.

Mandating a "solution" to Covid, but not coming up with solutions to other health problems which cause a higher number of deaths than Covid is weird. How about we mandate exercise or mandate the kind of food people eat to reduce the number of heart attacks?

If Covid vaccines hadn't caused injuries and were effective, in other words, if they were safe and effective, I imagine many fewer people would be "vaccine hesitant". And it stands now, we are mandating people assume risk, which is immoral.

In the next chapter we will look at excess deaths in the 25-44 year old age group and see how many deaths could be attributed to Covid.

# 14... Excess Mortality: age 25-44

*"By now the eradication of Western cultural wealth was largely complete. By now it was generally accepted that people could fully police others' behavior, and other people's bodies. And that mean the end of the Western tradition of the sovereign individual with free will, who decides for him or herself, but also understands that his or her will cannot be imposed on others who are not directly harming him or her. It heads squarely into the collectivist assumption in which third parties' bodies are legitimately policed."* p. 285
The Body of Others by Naomi Wolf

Naomi Wolf (1962-) is an author, a journalist and a business owner. Her most recent book is "The Body of others". In 2007 she wrote the best-selling book "The End of America".

In this chapter my goal is to show you the HUGE increase in excess death in the 25-44 year old age group in the US from 2020 to 2021. My hope is that you wonder what caused the non-Covid deaths in this working age population.

Now let's focus on the group that has seen the highest number of excess deaths out of all of the age groups in the US: the 25-44 year olds.

Let's compare the number of deaths involving Covid to the number of deaths not related to Covid in their age group in 2020 and 2021.

According to the CDC, over 50% of the 25-44 year old age group were fully vaccinated by June 24<sup>th</sup> 2021 and their age group comprised roughly 5% of all Covid deaths in the US in 2020 when there were no Covid vaccines. Recall this chart:

## US: Deaths from all causes and Covid related deaths-2020

| Age | Approximate population | Total deaths from all causes | Total number of Deaths involving Covid | % of deaths involving Covid out of total deaths |
|---|---|---|---|---|
| 0-17 | 71.3 million | 34,204 | 199 | 0.6% |
| 18-29 | 48.8 million | 63,520 | 1,489 | 2.3% |
| 30-39 | 44.7 million | 89,319 | 4,294 | 4.8% |
| 40-49 | 40.3 million | 133,464 | 11,336 | 8.5% |
| 50-64 | 62.8 million | 557,214 | 56,802 | 10.2% |
| 65-74 | 32.5 million | 675,940 | 82,332 | 12.2% |
| 75-84 | 16.5 million | 823,038 | 106,319 | 12.9% |
| 85+ | 6.7 million | 1,013,340 | 122,895 | 12.1% |

Looking at the *All Cause Excess Mortality* chart for people age 25-44 below, you can see that this group has suffered <u>a huge number </u>of excess deaths. Excess deaths are signified by the solid trend line. I put in vertical lines to mark the years 2021 and 2022.

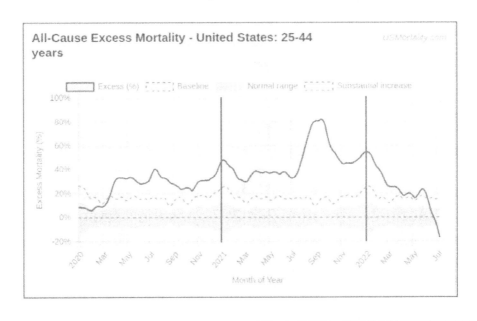

Notice how there was a huge death wave that started in July 2021 and ended in November 2021. The wave reached 80% excess mortality That 80% plateau lasted from late August 2021 to early October 2021- for about 6 weeks. July and August coincide with the time that huge numbers of college students, faculty and staff were getting vaccinated to go back to college and university campuses face to face. I'm not saying they died due to taking Covid vaccines. Rather, the timing coincides.

**Cumulative excess deaths – US 25-44 year olds**
Here is the running total of how many excess deaths occurred in the 25-44 year old age group in 2020, 2021 and 2022 from USMortality:

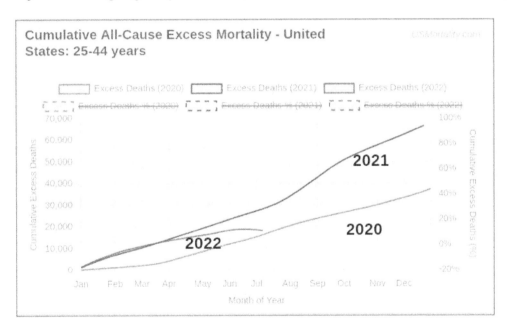

There were far more excess deaths in 2021 than in 2020. There were more excess deaths (Jan-July) in 2022 than at this time in 2020. USMortality reports the increase in deaths in the 25-44 age group. (I copy their words exactly + bolding is mine):

**2020**: United States reported **181,422** deaths of 25-44 years for the year 2020. Expected deaths were **144,088.** That is an increase of **37,334** deaths **(+25.9%)**.

**2021**: United States reported **208,027** deaths of 25-44 years for the year 2021. Expected deaths were **141,466**. That is an increase of **66,561** deaths **(+47.1%)**.

**2022**: To date, for the year 2022, United States reported **89,662** deaths of 25-44 years ages. Expected deaths thus far, were **73,047**. That is an increase of 16,615 deaths **(+22.7%)**.
Let's see what those numbers look like in a table:

**US Deaths: Age 25-44**

| Year | Deaths expected | Deaths reported | Excess deaths | Percent increase in deaths |
|------|-----------------|-----------------|---------------|----------------------------|
| 2020 | 144,048 | 181,422 | 37,334 | **+25.9%** |
| 2021 | 141,466 | 208,027 | 66,561 | **+47.1%** |
| 2022 | 73,047 | 89,662 | 16,615 | **+22.7%** |

There were so many excess deaths in 2020 (37,334) and in 2021 (66,561), and through August 17th 2022 (16,615)! We don't expect 25-44 year olds to die. Let's go to the CDC to figure out how many of these excess deaths can be attributed to Covid. Recall that in 2020, 25-44 year olds made up about 5% of all Covid related deaths. A problem arises when capturing the exact number of Covid-related deaths for the 25-44 year olds because US Mortality breaks down the ages differently from the CDC and this required extrapolation.

**Age Breakdown**

| US Mortality | CDC |
|--------------|-----|
| 25-44 | 18-29 |
| 45-64 | 30-39 |
| | 40-49 |
| | 50-64 |

For example, to capture the Covid related deaths in the 25-44 year age group, I had to span three age groups. I had to look at the CDC's 18-29 year old category to get 5 years of data (age 25-29). So, to estimate the number of deaths for 25-29 year olds, I multiplied the total number of Covid related deaths in the 18-29 age group by **0.42.** (18-24 is 7 years. 25-29 is 5 years. 5 / 12 = 0.42) For the 40-49 year old age group I divided the number of deaths by 2. The numbers aren't exact, but still paint a startling picture.

Here is a screen shot from the CDC: The total number of Deaths involving Covid in age group 18-49. Again, we are looking at the 25-44 year olds, so extrapolation is required. (Retrieved Aug 17, 2022):

| State | | | Sex |
|---|---|---|---|
| United States | | | Multiple sele |
| Year in which death occurred | Sex | Age Group | All Deaths involving COVID-19 [1] |
| 2022 | All Sexes | 18-29 years | 1,074 |
| 2022 | All Sexes | 30-39 years | 2,816 |
| 2022 | All Sexes | 40-49 years | 6,432 |
| 2021 | All Sexes | 18-29 years | 3,933 |
| 2021 | All Sexes | 30-39 years | 11,575 |
| 2021 | All Sexes | 40-49 years | 26,214 |
| 2020 | All Sexes | 18-29 years | 1,489 |
| 2020 | All Sexes | 30-39 years | 4,294 |
| 2020 | All Sexes | 40-49 years | 11,336 |

Now, let's try to account for the number of excess deaths. Did more people age 25-44 die from a Covid infection or from something else?

**Accounting for the excess deaths (age 25-44) … Covid or not?**

| Year | Excess deaths | Number of deaths involving Covid | Number of non-Covid deaths |
|---|---|---|---|
| 2020 | 37,334 | 10,587 | 26,747 |
| 2021 | 66,561 | 26,334 | 40,227 |
| 2022 (Aug 17) | 16,615 | 6,483 | 10,132 |

Covid infections did not account for the majority of excess deaths in 2020, 2021 or 2022. The media had presented Covid to us in such a scary way in 2020 and 2021 that I had assumed the vast majority of excess deaths would be attributed to a Covid infection.

Look at the number of excess deaths each year: 2020-**37,334**; 2021-**66,561** and 2022- **16,615.** In total, **29,227** more people died in 2021 than in 2020 in the 25-44 year old age group. Taken together 2020-2021, there were **43,404** Covid related deaths and **77,106** non-Covid deaths. To account for the excess deaths, **64%** were non-Covid and **36%** were related to Covid even by virtue of people dying of something else and testing positive for Covid. Also, in 2021 roughly **16,000 more deaths** involved Covid than we saw in 2020 despite over half of the 25-44 year olds being vaccinated by June 24th 2021.

Why did things get markedly worse for the 25-44 age group in 2021? What caused the dramatic increases in both Covid and non-Covid deaths? We should have seen fewer Covid-related deaths in 2021 due to vaccination. However, we have to remember that in 2020 we had roughly 9 months of Covid compared to 2021 when we had 12. Compare the 9 months of Covid deaths in 2020 (10,587) to the 12 months of Covid related deaths in 2021 (26,334). About **2.5 times** more Covid related deaths occurred in 2021 than in 2020.

Adjusting for time (9 months to 9 months) if we subtract 25% of the Covid related deaths in 2021, and we still see a significant increase in Covid related deaths: adjusted Covid related deaths in 2021 = **19,751** compared to **10,587** in 2020. Let's look again at the excess death numbers. This time as percentages:

**Accounting for excess deaths: Covid v Non-Covid (age 25-44)**

| Year | Excess deaths | % of deaths involving Covid | % of non-Covid deaths |
|------|---------------|-----------------------------|-----------------------|
| 2020 | 37,334 | 28% | 72% |
| 2021 | 66,561 | 40% | 60% |
| 2022 | 16,615 | 39% | 61% |

Let's think about the answers to these questions:

-What factors were different in people's lives compared to 2019 that caused these excess deaths?

-What caused the number of Deaths involving Covid to **increase by 78%** from 2020 to 2021? (37,334 v 66,561)

-Was the massive increase in deaths involving Covid in 2021 due to increased deaths in unvaccinated people?

- Is the test used to determine if a person had a Covid death reliable?

Many doctors and scientists have been looking into the issue of excess deaths. In the article ***What Is the Cause of Increased Mortality Rates? - Emerging statistics on excess mortality rates paint an alarming picture*** (September 2nd 2022) Dr. Mercola writes:

*"In the US., we lost 349,000 younger Americans to something besides COVID-19 (deaths in total, not just excess) and non-natural death between April 3 and Aug. 13, and that's not counting the tens of thousands of death records that the CDC has inexplicably deleted.*

---

*As much as 15% to 25% of the death reports that could indicate a COVID-19 jab death are missing. Other data show that during the fall of 2021,* **Millennials, aged 25 to 44, had an 84% increase in excess deaths."**

Are government agencies and pro-vaccine doctors and other pro-vaccine people examining these claims or are they just not curious? Are they even willing to look?

Why did so many people die in 2021? It's newsworthy. If Covid vaccines are associated with <u>any</u> deaths shouldn't that be told to us?

Denmark has a sensible Covid vaccine policy. For one, they do not recommend vaccination for people under the age of 50. According to the Danish health authority (my underlining):

*"The Danish Health Authority expects that the number of Covid-19 infections will increase during autumn and winter. Therefore, <u>we recommend</u> vaccination of people <u>aged 50 years and over </u>as well as selected risk groups. Read more about the autumn vaccination program here…The risk of becoming severely ill from Covid-19 increases with age. Therefore, people who have reached the age of 50 and particularly vulnerable people will be <u>offered vaccination</u>. We expect that many people will be infected with Covid-19 during autumn and winter. It is therefore important that the population remembers the guidance on how to prevent infection, which also applies to a number of other infectious diseases."*

I like their words: recommend, offered. And I doubt that a huge segment of the Danish population would be in favor of segregating and discriminating against the unvaccinated.

In the next chapter we will look at <u>the total number of deaths</u> (not just excess deaths) among 25-44 year olds comparing 2020 to 2021.

# 15... Deaths age 25-44: Comparing 2020 to 2021

*"… when people rolled up their sleeve, my word, they were trusting. I read the packages, and I said I am not going to have this stuff… When they say the CV19 vax is safe, I say you have no idea if it is safe. You have literally not done the experiments."*

- Dr. Michael Yeadon (age unknown) was the former Pfizer VP & Chief Scientific Officer, and a Biochemistry and Toxicology specialist. He oversaw the development of drugs for asthma and holds a PhD in Respiratory Pharmacology.

In this chapter my goal is to look at the total number of deaths in the 25-44 year old age group that occurred in 2020 and 2021 and to show the percentage of people who had a death involving Covid out of the entire 25-44 year old population. If Covid isn't a big risk to that group, and if the Covid vaccines come with risks and don't work as we had promised, why are they mandated? Moreover, what is causing so many extra deaths?

In the last chapter, we looked at excess deaths and how many could be attributed to Covid. Now, let's look at the **total number of deaths** in the 25-44 year old age group and compare the number of deaths from all causes and from Covid in 2020 to 2021. Did the total number of deaths increase or decrease?

How big of a risk is a death related to Covid in the 25-44 year old age group when you take into account their population?

Below is an image from the CDC showing the total deaths from all causes and deaths involving Covid in 2020 and 2021 for the age groups: 18-29, 30-39 and 30-49.

| State | | | Sex | |
|-------|--|--|-----|--|
| United States ▽ | | | Multiple sele... ▽ | |

| Year in which death occurred ▼ | Sex | Age Group | All Deaths involving COVID-19 [1] | Deaths from All Causes |
|---|---|---|---|---|
| 2021 | All Sexes | 18-29 years | 3,933 | 68,114 |
| 2021 | All Sexes | 30-39 years | 11,575 | 104,177 |
| 2021 | All Sexes | 40-49 years | 26,214 | 155,548 |
| | | | | |
| 2020 | All Sexes | 18-29 years | 1,489 | 63,520 |
| 2020 | All Sexes | 30-39 years | 4,294 | 89,319 |
| 2020 | All Sexes | 40-49 years | 11,336 | 133,464 |

Extrapolation:

I multiply the numbers in the 18-29 year old group by 0.42.

I divide the numbers in the 40-49 year old group by 2.

*The numbers are therefore approximate.

## Total Deaths: Covid + Not-Covid related in 25-44 year olds

| Year | Population | Total Deaths all Causes | Deaths involving Covid | Deaths from non-Covid causes |
|------|-----------|------------------------|------------------------|------------------------------|
| 2020 | 67,196,000 | 182,729 | 10,587 | 172,142 |
| 2021 | | 210,559 | 26,335 | 184,224 |

In 2020, **0.27%** of the 25-44 age group died from any cause. In 2021 approximately **0.31%** died from any cause.

In 2020, **0.016%** of the 25-44 age group had a death involving Covid. In 2021 approximately **0.04%** had a death involving Covid.

As stated in the last chapter, but I think worthy of repeating: In 2021 approximately **26,335** died from Covid related causes...a near **150%** increase from 2020 despite over half of that population being fully vaccinated. Adjusting for time (9 months to 9 months), we still see a significant increase in Covid related deaths: 2021 adjusted Covid related deaths = **19,751** compared to **10,587** in 2020, a near **87%** increase. Doesn't an 87% increase seem weird when over half of the population got a Covid vaccine?

Let's return to the total death chart to see the percentage of deaths involving Covid and the percentage of deaths from non-Covid causes:

## Total Deaths: Covid + Not-Covid related in 25-44 year olds

| Year | Population | Total Deaths all Causes | Deaths involving Covid | Deaths from non-Covid causes |
|------|-----------|------------------------|------------------------|------------------------------|
| 2020 | | 182,729 | 5.8% | 94.2% |
| 2021 | 67,196,000 | 210,559 | 12.5% | 87.5% |

There was a significant **15%** increase in total deaths from all causes from 2020 (182,729) to 2021 (210,559). A 15% increase in deaths from all causes is shocking. Life insurance companies say that a 10% rise happens only in about 1 in 200 years. Many of us who have been researching Covid since March 2020 wonder if the vaccines could be associated with the huge increases in deaths.

In the article ***Further evidence of mRNA injections associated with both COVID deaths and excess non-COVID deaths. Re-analysis of deaths of 18 to 55 year olds in the USA,*** author Joe Smally (Pro Bono COVID data analysis for legal challenges) writes (my underlining):

*"...mRNA experiment <u>could be held accountable for one-third of non-COVID excess deaths based on results showing a statistically significant relationship between mRNA dosing rates and deaths 23 weeks later.</u> Of course, this corroborates the work of Steve Kirsch as well… The burning question recently is - are these non-COVID excess deaths due to the mRNA experiment, lockdowns and everything associated with them, or something else? Perhaps, even under-diagnosed COVID deaths?*

*The pro-vax camp have done everything they can to pin it on interventions (<u>without actually putting forward any evidence to support the presumption</u>). I guess it's easier to maintain that this is just the collateral damage of all the millions of lives they saved from COVID? It also means, they can carry on milking the mRNA cow (until her udders bleed). Given that the sacred cow doesn't feed me, I have no constraints in investigating any possible relationship between the mRNA and excess deaths... These deaths should be considered in the context of risk benefit. If the lives saved by the mRNA experiment are substantially higher than the deaths caused then this should be taken into consideration."*

Don't you agree?

In the article ***Scientists from Harvard & Johns Hopkins Found Covid-19 Vaccines 98 Times Worse Than the Virus*** by Steve Kirsch (September 12th 2022), Kirsch quotes from the Harvard and John Hopkins study and shares his thoughts. (my underlining):

*"Using CDC and sponsor-reported adverse event data, we find that booster mandates may cause a net expected harm: per COVID-19 hospitalization prevented in previously uninfected young adults, we anticipate 18 to 98 serious adverse events, including 1.7 to 3.0 booster-associated myocarditis cases in males, and 1,373 to 3,234 cases of grade ≥3 reactogenicity which interferes with daily activities. Given the high prevalence of post-infection immunity, this risk-benefit profile is even less favorable."*

Kirsch's comment: *"If this doesn't cause all universities worldwide to drop the vaccine mandates, I don't know what will. It should also shatter confidence in the CDC and cause investigations to take place."*

All Covid vaccine mandates should be dropped. The risks that accompany Covid vaccines should have been made available to each person before injection and broadcast widely in media to the public at large.

Finally, according to VAERS, the Vaccine Adverse Events Reporting System, in the 25-44 age group **539** death reports were filed related to Covid vaccines in the US through September 13th 2022. Vaccine associated injuries and deaths are vastly **under-reported**, not over-reported.

The mainstream media has been dismissive toward VAERS, which angers me. Every life lost or injured reported to VAERS deserves investigation, recognition and remedy to the loved ones left behind.

Here are three VAERS reports of death in young people shortly after Covid vaccination. (The reports are very hard to read, so I summarize each):

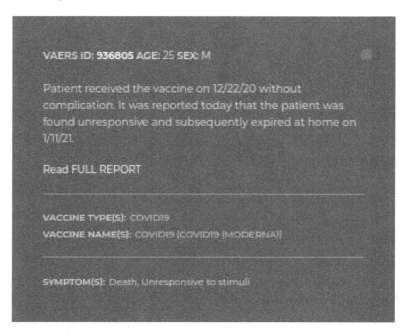

VAERS ID: **936805** AGE: 25 SEX: M

Patient received the vaccine on 12/22/20 without complication. It was reported today that the patient was found unresponsive and subsequently expired at home on 1/11/21.

Read FULL REPORT

VACCINE TYPE(S): COVID19
VACCINE NAME(S): COVID19 (COVID19 (MODERNA))

SYMPTOM(S): Death, Unresponsive to stimuli

This death was a 25 year old male. He got a vaccine on 12/22/20 and was found dead at home on 1/11/21. Here's another report:

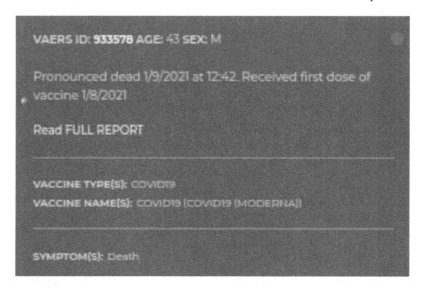

VAERS ID: **933578** AGE: 43 SEX: M

Pronounced dead 1/9/2021 at 12:42. Received first dose of vaccine 1/8/2021

Read FULL REPORT

VACCINE TYPE(S): COVID19
VACCINE NAME(S): COVID19 (COVID19 (MODERNA))

SYMPTOM(S): Death

This death occurred in a 43 year old male. He received his first dose of a Covid vaccine on 1/8/21 and died on 1/9/21.

Here's the report of a 33 year old female:

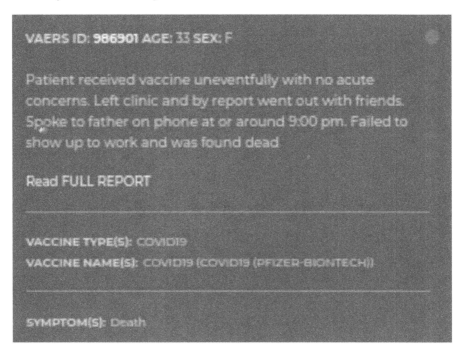

VAERS ID: **986901** AGE: 33 SEX: F

Patient received vaccine uneventfully with no acute concerns. Left clinic and by report went out with friends. Spoke to father on phone at or around 9:00 pm. Failed to show up to work and was found dead

Read FULL REPORT

VACCINE TYPE(S): COVID19
VACCINE NAME(S): COVID19 (COVID19 (PFIZER-BIONTECH))

SYMPTOM(S): Death

This 33 year old woman received her vaccine, and then went out with friends, and talked to her dad on the phone at 9:00 pm. She failed to show up for work the next day. She was found dead.

These deaths need to be looked into seriously.

In the next chapter we will look at the huge increase in the amount of money paid out in death benefits by life insurance companies and the growing funeral business.

# 16... Life insurance companies and the Funeral Business

*"The reality is that you will grieve forever. You will not 'get over' the loss of a loved one; you will learn to live with it. You will heal and you will rebuild yourself around the loss you have suffered. You will be whole again but you will never be the same. Nor should you be the same nor would you want to."* – Elisabeth Kübler-Ross

In this chapter my goal is to show you what life insurance companies and what funeral businesses are saying about the increase in deaths. I hope you get the sense that we are facing a huge problem that isn't being widely discussed in mainstream media.

Life insurance companies noticed the huge increase in deaths in the US in 2020 and 2021 that we saw in the last chapter. The chart: ***All-Cause Excess Mortality – United States*** is thanks to USMortality:

Life insurance is a big business. They want you to pay your premiums, and they don't want you to die. That way they can make a profit, taking in more money in premiums than they have to pay out in death benefits. Some workplaces offer life insurance policies to their employees. These policies are known as group life insurance policies.

In the chart below you can see the increase in deaths from all causes (including Covid-related deaths) from 2020 to 2021. Significant increases in death occurred in all age groups except for the 85+ age group.

This huge increase in death has heavily impacted the life insurance industry.

**% change in # of deaths from all causes from 2020 to 2021**

| 0-17 | 18-29 | 30-39 | 40-49 | 50-64 | 65-74 | 75-84 | 85+ |
|------|-------|-------|-------|-------|-------|-------|-----|
| +4.6% | +7.2% | +16.6% | +16.5% | +9.5% | +7.5% | +0.9% | -7.1% |

Recall that Covid was not the majority of excess deaths in the 25-44 year old age group.

Notice how the biggest increases in deaths occurred in the 30-39 (16.6%) and the 40-49 (16.5%) age groups. How was 2021 different from 2020?

1) The Covid-19 virus

2) Covid-related mandates causing job loss, economic problems and stress

3) Putting off needed medical care due to the lockdowns

4) Covid vaccines in 2021

It boils down to this: Was it the virus, the government's response to the virus or Covid vaccination which caused these deaths?

**Life Insurance Companies**

Life insurance companies in the US were alarmed by the huge increase in death. From 2020 to 2021, the insurance company *Lincoln National* reported a **163% increase** in the amount of money they paid out in death benefits, and these deaths were mostly NOT related to Covid. From the June 15th 2022 article (below) we read:

"...Lincoln National attributes the $41 million operating loss to "non-pandemic-related morbidity" and "unusual claims adjustments.""

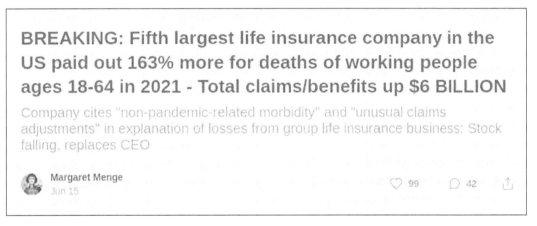

The huge increases in non-Covid deaths has been written about in independent media. However, I don't see it being discussed on the TV news or in the papers. Isn't such a dramatic increase in death newsworthy?

Here are the amounts of money paid out in death benefits by *Lincoln National* from 2019-2021:

**2019**: $500,888,808

**2020**: $547,940,260

**2021**: $1,445,350,949

Looking at the rise in death benefits paid out from 2019 ($500,888,808) to 2020 ($547,940,260) it is a reasonable assumption that the Covid virus was responsible for the **9.4%** increase in death benefit payouts.

However, what accounted for the dramatic **163%** increase in life insurance payouts from 2020 to 2021?

Here is another life insurance company, *OneAmerica,* that also took notice of the increase in deaths. In the January 3rd 2022 article **OneAmerica Insurance CEO: Deaths Increase 40% Among People Ages 18-64** we read:

*"We are seeing, right now, the highest death rates we have seen in the history of this business – not just at OneAmerica,"... The data is consistent across every player in that business... Just to give you an idea of how bad that is… a one-in-200-year catastrophe would be 10% increase over pre-pandemic. So 40% is just unheard of…"*

The 163% jump in life insurance payouts at *Lincoln National* doesn't make sense to me and neither does the 40% increase at *OneAmerica*. Does it make sense to you? We need to know what caused the increase in death in 2021.

**Group Life COVID-19 Mortality Survey Report**
Because the huge increase in death has rocked the life insurance industry, in August 2022 a survey was carried out by the *Group Life Experience Committee of the Society of Actuaries* to gather information about these deaths. Twenty of the top 21 US group term life insurance companies participated in the survey.

Below is a chart showing the total claims per 1,000 people by month and year. Notice the huge increase in death claims in 2020, 2021 and 2022 compared to 2017-2019:

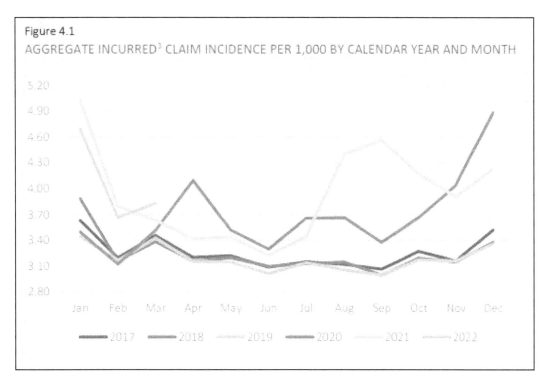

Figure 4.1
AGGREGATE INCURRED[3] CLAIM INCIDENCE PER 1,000 BY CALENDAR YEAR AND MONTH

In 2020 the most death claims were in December at 4.9 per 1,000 policy holders.

In January 2021 there were approximately 5.0 death claims per 1,000 policy holders. Later, there was a steep rise in death claims from July to August 2021. What caused those deaths? Then there was a more gradual increase from August to September 2021 reaching 4.6 death claims per 1,000. The peak in September 2021 was followed by a gradual decrease until November.

There were massive numbers of people getting vaccinated in the spring and summer of 2021. There looks to be an association between high levels of death and meeting vaccine mandate deadlines at colleges and universities, state agencies, the military and big companies. People who work for such places are also likely to have group life insurance policies as well. In 2022 most death claims per 1,000 occurred in January at over 4.6. They fell sharply until February and then increased gradually until March (when the recording ends.)

The increase in deaths in August-December 2021 also coincides with a Covid death wave as well. Let's see what we can determine by comparing the Covid death wave peaks and the peaks in life insurance claims starting in 2020 and going through March 2022 (I will also talk about the squares in the charts):

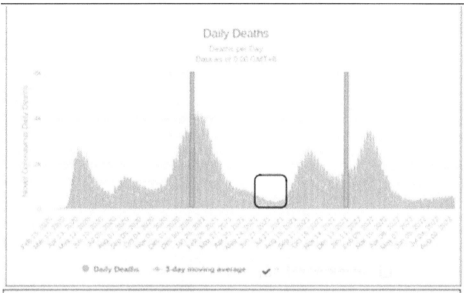

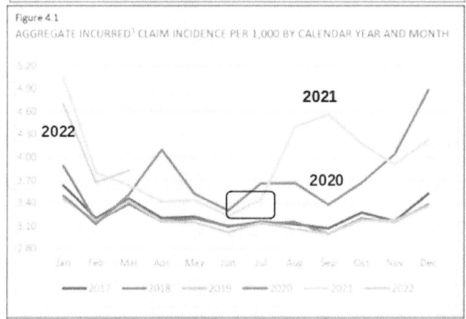

Figure 4.1
AGGREGATE INCURRED[1] CLAIM INCIDENCE PER 1,000 BY CALENDAR YEAR AND MONTH

1- There was a peak in Covid related deaths in April 2020. There was a peak in life insurance claims as well.

2- There was peak in Covid related deaths in December 2020. There was a peak in life insurance claims as well.

3- In September 2021 there was a peak in Covid related deaths. There was a peak in life insurance claims as well.

4- I wonder why there were so many more death claims in August and September of 2021 compared to August and September of 2020 when there was no vaccine.

5- A difference can be seen when comparing the two charts: In the Covid death chart there was a decrease in deaths from June to July 2021 while in the life insurance claims chart there was an increase in deaths from June to July 2021. (signified difference with squares.)

It's a little morbid to think about and investigate why so many more life insurance holders were dying in 2021 than in 2020. But I think it is necessary. We need brave journalists to report on the number of excess deaths that have occurred. As a resource, they could read and report on the **Group Life COVID-19 Mortality Survey Report**.

From that report, here is a chart comparing the percentage of excess deaths in the life insurance policy holder group to the percentage of excess deaths in the total US population by quarter:

Table 2.5
GROUP LIFE AND U.S. POPULATION EXCESS MORTALITY PERCENTAGES BY QUARTER

| Age | Q2 2020 | Q3 2020 | Q4 2020 | Q1 2021 | Q2 2021 | Q3 2021 | Q4 2021 | Q1 2022 |
|---|---|---|---|---|---|---|---|---|
| Group Life | 16% | 15% | 28% | 23% | 7% | 34% | 25% | 20% |
| U.S. Population | 20% | 16% | 26% | 17% | 6% | 24% | 20% | 18% |
| Difference | -4% | -1% | 2% | 6% | 1% | 10% | 5% | 2% |

The highest percentage of excess deaths in the group life insurance group occurred in the third quarter of 2021 at **34%** (high levels of vaccination in the life insurance holders group because of mandates) while the highest percentage of excess deaths in the US population occurred in the fourth quarter of 2020 at **26%** (no vaccination).

Yes, I am suspicious.

The second and third quarters of 2020 saw higher percentages of excess deaths in the US population than in the group life insurance population. People who have life insurance policies tend to be richer than people who don't. More wealth correlates with better health.

Doesn't it make sense that a group of people who were highly vaccinated would have been protected from a Covid related death than the general US population who were less vaccinated?

Yet, returning to the third quarter of 2021, we see a huge difference in their percentage of excess deaths. For life insurance holders, it was **34%** versus the US population was **24%**. This represents a near **42%** higher level of excess deaths in the insured population compared to the US population!

Incidentally, OpenVAERS reports **3,314** deaths associated with Covid vaccines in 24-65 year olds nationwide as of October 2nd 2022. Is this being addressed by the FDA, CDC, our government officials and mainstream journalists?

Finally, below is a chart showing the **causes** of death per 1,000 insurance claims:

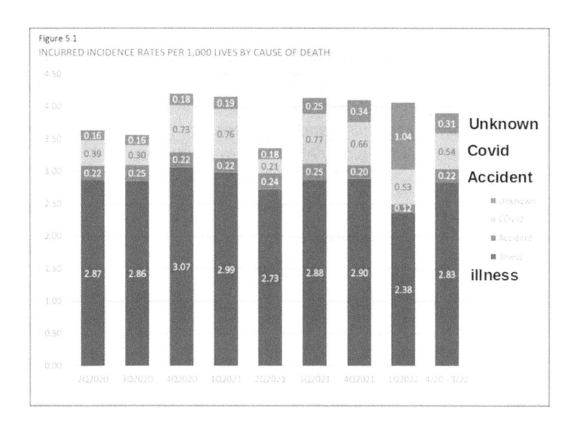

Figure 5.1
INCURRED INCIDENCE RATES PER 1,000 LIVES BY CAUSE OF DEATH

Recall from the chart before this, that the highest level of excess death in the insured population occurred in the third quarter of 2021 at **34%**. The greatest number of Covid-related deaths occurred in three quarters: the fourth quarter of 2020 (0.73), the first quarter of 2021 (0.76) and the third quarter of 2021 (0.77).

Also and interestingly, from the third quarter of 2021 there were higher levels of deaths from unknown causes than in the previous five quarters. The greatest number of deaths due to unknown causes occurred in the first quarter of 2022 at 1.04, over three times as many as had occurred in the fourth quarter of 2021 at 0.34. The fourth quarter of 2021 had the second highest number of deaths due to unknown causes.

What could those unknown causes be?

## Funeral Homes

The funeral services industry has had a huge increase in demand. In this image one funeral company, **Service Corporation International**, which touts itself as *"...North America's leading provider of funeral, cremation and cemetery services"*, is essentially telling its investors not to worry about future dividends:

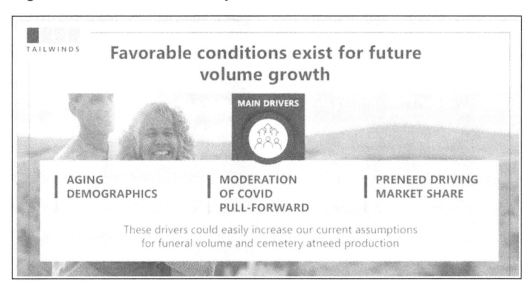

*"Favorable conditions exist for future volume growth"* (Oh….Why?)

Since the start of the Covid era, Alex Berenson, a former NY Times journalist, has devoted a lot of time studying the government's response to Covid, including the Covid vaccines, masks and lockdowns and writing articles which he publishes on Substack.

In the August 5th 2022 article **The Funeral Business is doing great!** Berenson writes about a presentation given to investors and Wall Street analysts by Tom Ryan, the CEO of *Service Corporation International*. In Mr. Ryan's words with Berenson's comments:

*"... So like we tried to point out at investor day, I think we're experiencing -- we're servicing elevated numbers of consumers.* [Or, in English, having more funerals and cremations.]

*And you'd say, OK, what is that, Tom? Well, we've mentioned a little bit, we think there's still excess deaths. We think we can correlate it with lack of healthcare, people probably drinking too much, smoking too much, driving too fast, depression and access to mental health"*

Berenson comments: *"The problem with Tom's explanation about the causes of the excess is that none of them make sense. Smoking and obesity take decades to kill, and drinking usually takes a decade or more. Overdoses are way up and traffic accidents are higher too, but not nearly enough to account for the overall rise in deaths."*

Berenson's comments make sense. Smoking, obesity and drinking won't make a huge segment of the population die at the same three month period of time.

People who work in the funeral industry are speaking out too. Here is what a commenter who works at a funeral home wrote in response to the YouTube video **Spike in Sudden Adult Death Syndrome" (SADS) & Experts are BAFFLED as to WHY!**:

*"...I work in a funeral home and commented on previous posts that this was happening. I was told by colleagues, friends, and family (some of which are medical doctors); that this phenomenon was not occurring. In one week we did funeral for 38 yr old male, 37 yrs male and 29 yrs female. All died suddenly 2 were found at home, one at work. And others dying while doing yoga on vacations etc. I had 2 past colleagues die suddenly; one in there sleep and one from a massive heart attack which they survived, but didn't survive the stroke. I'm collecting data as we speak."*

The deaths due to unknown causes or in higher than usual numbers in both the insurance industry and the funeral industry need to be investigated by all people who are writing policies mandating Covid vaccination and by those enforcing vaccination, by the CDC and FDA, by governments nationwide as well as by every elected official.

Again, the numbers I have presented need to be dug into by statisticians and mathematicians, those without a bias.

If you are looking for an investment opportunity it might be better to put your money in the funeral business rather than the life insurance business. That said, I am not a certified financial planner, so don't take my advice.

It is questionable how well the Covid vaccine works in keeping people alive.

In the next chapter we look at the highest vaccinated groups and how they fared when facing the 2021 Covid death wave compared to the death waves in 2020 when there were no Covid vaccines.

# 17... Vaccinated groups face 2021 Covid-related death wave

*"No one can confidently say that he will still be living tomorrow"* – Euripides (484-407 BCE) was one of the greatest writers of Greek tragedies and wrote 90 plays. Euripides was also famous for asking people awkward questions.

In this chapter my goal is to show that Covid vaccination seemed to protect the 75-84 and 85+ age groups, but not the 65-74 age group from the July-December 2021 Covid death wave. It is my hope that you will agree with me that the decision to take a Covid vaccine should be left up to the individual.

**Waves of Death**

Again, there were 5 waves of Covid-related deaths between March of 2020 and August 2022. This chart of daily Covid related deaths is from *Worldometer*.

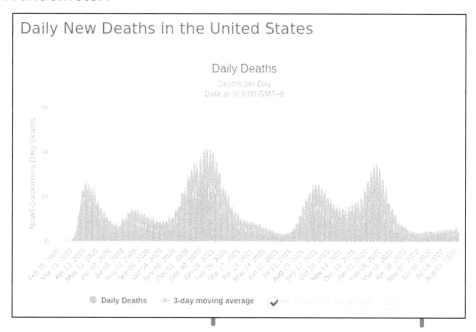

## Vaccination Rates

A full 81% of people over the age of 65 were fully vaccinated by June 24th 2021. So the vast majority of people over the age of 65 should be well protected from the July – December 2021 Covid death wave.

| Age | % Fully Vaccinated |
|---|---|
| 5-11 | 0.4% |
| 12-17 | 26.3% |
| 18-24 | 41.3% |
| 25-49 | 50.4% |
| 50-64 | 66.7% |
| 65 | 81.0% |

In the chart, I put in horizontal lines to roughly indicate the July – December time time frames.

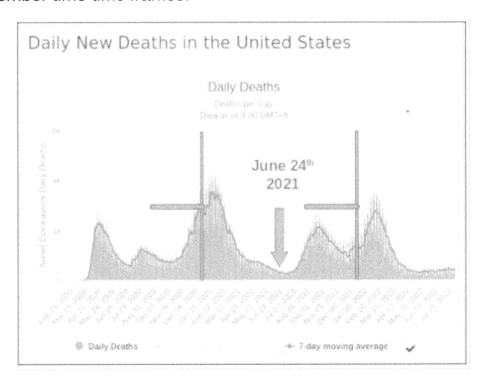

Now, let's turn to the number of people age 65+ who had a death involving Covid in July-December 2020 and then look at the number of people age 65+ who had a Covid related death in July-December 2021.

Did fewer older people die in 2021 because they were vaccinated?

**July-December 2020**

In 2020 the three oldest groups in the US were unvaccinated and there was a total of **208,401** deaths involving Covid from July-December 2020. (Numbers from the CDC.)

| Age | Vaccination rate | Deaths involving Covid July-Dec 2020 |
|---|---|---|
| 65-74 | 0 | 55,310 |
| 75-84 | 0 | 72,390 |
| 85+ | 0 | 80,701 |

**July-December 2021**

From July – December 2021 there was a total of **149,861** deaths involving Covid in the 3 oldest age groups who were highly vaccinated, which represents a significant **28% decrease** in deaths involving Covid from July-December 2020 in these age groups.

| Age | Vaccination rate | Deaths involving Covid July-Dec 2021 |
|---|---|---|
| 65-74 | 81% | 59,084 |
| 75-84 | 81% | 51,598 |
| 85+ | 81% | 39,179 |

Below is table showing the percent of change in the number of deaths from July-December 2020 to July-December 2021 by age group.

| Age | Vaccination rate | Deaths involving Covid July-Dec 2020 | Deaths involving Covid July-Dec 2021 | % change |
|---|---|---|---|---|
| 65-74 | 81% | 55,310 | 59,084 | +6.8% |
| 75-84 | 81% | 72,390 | 51,598 | -28.7% |
| 85+ | 81% | 80,701 | 39,179 | -51% |

Comparing July-December 2020 to July-December 2021, the risk – benefit analysis of Covid vaccination might weigh in favor of the oldest populations in the US (75-84) and (85+) getting vaccinated. People age 75-84 saw a **28.7%** drop in deaths involving Covid and the 85+ group saw a **51%** drop. However, the 65-74 year old group saw an increase of **+6.8%** in deaths involving Covid despite a high level of vaccination at **81%**. Why is that? It doesn't make sense in light of the huge drops in the other two populations.

I really would like an explanation.

To get a fuller picture of deaths during the July-December time frame in 2020 and 2021 let's look at the number of total deaths from all causes (including Covid) in the three age groups 65-74, 75-84 and 85+ to see if there was an increase or decrease in deaths from any cause in those age groups.

Remember, all groups were highly vaccinated in 2021, and we saw a dramatic decrease in Covid related deaths in the 75-84 and 85+ age groups and a 6.8% increase in the 65-74 age group.

I go to the CDC data base to get numbers:

*All deaths involving Covid-19* and *Deaths from all causes*.

Here are the deaths for ages 65-74: July-December 2020:

| Month in which death occurred | Sex | Age Group | All Deaths involving COVID-19 [1] | Deaths from All Causes |
|---|---|---|---|---|
| December 2020 | All Sexes | 65-74 years | 20,618 | 74,247 |
| November 2020 | All Sexes | 65-74 years | 11,027 | 60,818 |
| October 2020 | All Sexes | 65-74 years | 5,336 | 54,962 |
| September 2020 | All Sexes | 65-74 years | 4,360 | 51,666 |
| August 2020 | All Sexes | 65-74 years | 6,902 | 55,992 |
| July 2020 | All Sexes | 65-74 years | 7,067 | 56,206 |

Here are the deaths for ages 65-74: July-December 2021:

| Month in which death occurred | Sex | Age Group | All Deaths involving COVID-19 [1] | Deaths from All Causes |
|---|---|---|---|---|
| December 2021 | All Sexes | 65-74 years | 11,555 | 67,664 |
| November 2021 | All Sexes | 65-74 years | 7,880 | 60,006 |
| October 2021 | All Sexes | 65-74 years | 10,460 | 63,091 |
| September 2021 | All Sexes | 65-74 years | 15,278 | 66,427 |
| August 2021 | All Sexes | 65-74 years | 11,374 | 63,832 |
| July 2021 | All Sexes | 65-74 years | 2,537 | 53,129 |

Here are the deaths for ages 75-84: July-December 2020:

| Month in which death occurred | Sex | Age Group | All Deaths involving COVID-19 [1] | Deaths from All Causes |
|---|---|---|---|---|
| December 2020 | All Sexes | 75-84 years | 28,153 | 92,913 |
| November 2020 | All Sexes | 75-84 years | 15,686 | 75,266 |
| October 2020 | All Sexes | 75-84 years | 7,133 | 66,562 |
| September 2020 | All Sexes | 75-84 years | 5,269 | 61,543 |
| August 2020 | All Sexes | 75-84 years | 8,092 | 66,667 |
| July 2020 | All Sexes | 75-84 years | 8,057 | 66,036 |

Here are the deaths for ages 75-84: July-December 2021:

| Month in which death occurred | Sex | Age Group | All Deaths involving COVID-19 [1] | Deaths from All Causes |
|---|---|---|---|---|
| December 2021 | All Sexes | 75-84 years | 10,729 | 78,158 |
| November 2021 | All Sexes | 75-84 years | 7,413 | 70,518 |
| October 2021 | All Sexes | 75-84 years | 8,761 | 70,897 |
| September 2021 | All Sexes | 75-84 years | 12,507 | 71,784 |
| August 2021 | All Sexes | 75-84 years | 9,821 | 70,189 |
| July 2021 | All Sexes | 75-84 years | 2,367 | 60,714 |

Here are the deaths for ages 85 +: July-December 2020:

| Month in which death occurred | Sex | Age Group | All Deaths involving COVID-19 [1] | Deaths from All Causes |
|---|---|---|---|---|
| December 2020 | All Sexes | 85 years and over | 32,831 | 113,288 |
| November 2020 | All Sexes | 85 years and over | 18,049 | 92,080 |
| October 2020 | All Sexes | 85 years and over | 8,082 | 80,791 |
| September 2020 | All Sexes | 85 years and over | 5,514 | 74,501 |
| August 2020 | All Sexes | 85 years and over | 8,092 | 78,566 |
| July 2020 | All Sexes | 85 years and over | 8,133 | 78,323 |

Here are the deaths for ages 85 + : July-December 2021:

| Month in which death occurred | Sex | Age Group | All Deaths involving COVID-19 [1] | Deaths from All Causes |
|---|---|---|---|---|
| December 2021 | All Sexes | 85 years and over | 8,202 | 87,129 |
| November 2021 | All Sexes | 85 years and over | 6,218 | 79,832 |
| October 2021 | All Sexes | 85 years and over | 7,005 | 79,559 |
| September 2021 | All Sexes | 85 years and over | 8,843 | 77,889 |
| August 2021 | All Sexes | 85 years and over | 7,076 | 77,571 |
| July 2021 | All Sexes | 85 years and over | 1,835 | 69,469 |

Recall the vaccination rates by June 24<sup>th</sup> 2021 and the deaths involving Covid:

| Age | Vaccination rate | Deaths involving Covid July-Dec 2020 | Deaths involving Covid July-Dec 2021 | % change |
|---|---|---|---|---|
| 65-74 | 81% | 55,310 | 59,084 | +6.8% |
| 75-84 | 81% | 72,390 | 51,598 | -28.7% |
| 85+ | 81% | 80,701 | 39,179 | -51% |

When we just look at just Covid-related deaths and don't examine all deaths, we are missing the non-Covid deaths. Dead is dead. Did more people over the age of 65 die (from any cause) July-December in 2021 or in July – December 2020?

**Total Deaths from all causes: July – Dec 2020 and 2021**

| Age | Population | Deaths from all causes 2020 | Deaths from all causes 2021 | Rate of change |
|---|---|---|---|---|
| 65-74 | 32.5 million | 353,891 | 374,149 | +5.7% |
| 75-84 | 16.5 million | 428,987 | 422,260 | -1.6% |
| 85+ | 6.7 million | 517,549 | 471,449 | -8.9% |

A **5.7%** increase in total deaths from all causes in the 65-74 year old group of 32.5 million people in July-December 2021 is substantial. Recall that the 65-74 year old age group also saw a **6.8%** increase in Covid-related deaths in July-December 2021, and their vaccination rate was **81%**. There were slightly fewer total deaths from all causes in the 75-84 year old group at -**1.6%** in July-December 2021 as well as a greater reduction in their Covid-related deaths at -**28.7%**. In the 85+ year old group there was an **8.9%** decrease in deaths in July-December 2021 and a huge decrease in Covid related deaths **51.0%**.

---

Now, let's compare the number of **non-Covid** deaths July-December 2020 to July-December 2021. This will tell us if more people died from things not related to Covid in 2021. (I subtracted the number of deaths involving Covid from the total number of deaths.)

**Non-Covid related deaths in the 3 oldest populations: July – December 2020 + 2021**

| Age | Population | Deaths from all causes minus Covid July-Dec 2020 | Deaths from all causes minus Covid July-Dec 2021 | Rate of Change |
|---|---|---|---|---|
| 65-74 | 32.5 million | 298,851 | 315,065 | +5.4% |
| 75-84 | 16.5 million | 356,597 | 370,662 | +3.9% |
| 85+ | 6.7 million | 436,848 | 432,270 | - 1.0% |

Subtracting the Covid-related deaths from the total deaths from all causes, there was an increase in deaths in the 65-74 year old age group (**+5.4%**) and in the 75-84 year old age group (**+3.9%**) The 85+ year old age group saw a decrease (**-1.0%**) in non-Covid deaths. I am interested in the rise in deaths not related to Covid. How many more non-Covid deaths occurred July to December 2021 than in July to December 2020 in the 65-74 age group and the 75-84 age group?

**The number of non-Covid deaths in 2021: age 65-74 and 75-84**

| Age | Population | Deaths from all causes minus Covid July-Dec 2020 | Deaths from all causes minus Covid July-Dec 2021 | Increase in the number of deaths from causes other than Covid in 2021 |
|---|---|---|---|---|
| 65-74 | 32.5 million | 298,851 | 315,065 | 16,214 |
| 75-84 | 16.5 million | 356,597 | 370,662 | 14,065 |

What caused 30,279 more deaths in July to December 2021 in people age 65-84?

According to OpenVAERS from January 2021 to September 23rd 2022, there were 6,872 deaths that were associated with Covid vaccines in the 65-84 age group which would account for nearly 23% of the non-Covid related death increase that occurred when comparing July and December 2020 and July-December 2021.

We see evidence of the link between Covid vaccination and death in the August 27th 2022 article ***Exhaustive study of German mortality data finds excess deaths tightly correlated with mass vaccination.*** In it we read about a study done by a psychologist and a statistician who analyzed all cause mortality data in Germany.

Here is a chart showing the excess mortality in Germany in 2020 and 2021. The age group is written along the X-axis and the % of excess mortality is written along the Y-axis

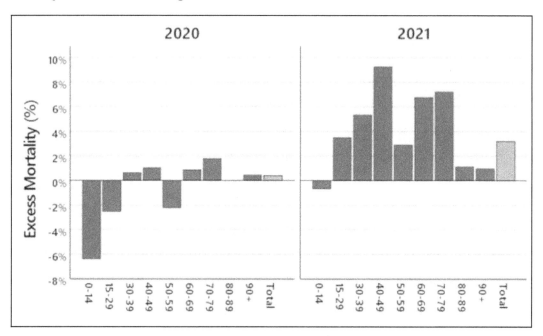

The author of the article analyzed the German study and wrote about what he learned. Here are some of the things he said:

*"...the mortality signal is very tightly correlated with the date of vaccination."*

*"The vaccines obviously do most of their harm by inducing adverse immune reactions, and thus they're relatively safe in the very elderly, who have weaker immune systems."*

*"The maybe most surprising fact is that [2021] produces in all age groups a significant mortality increase, which is in sharp contrast to the expectation that the vaccination should decrease the number of COVID-19 deaths. The only exception is the last age group [80+] …"*

*"It's no wonder that nothing—not lockdowns, not vaccines, not masks, not all the tests in the world—can drive down all-cause mortality in Germany."*

We have compared 2020 to 2021, do you understand why many people are concerned that Covid vaccines might be causing death?

In the next chapter we will look at how Covid vaccines correlate with injuries and death.

# 18... Do Covid vaccines increase injuries and deaths?

*'If only there were evil people somewhere insidiously committing evil deeds, it would be necessary only to separate them from the rest of us and destroy them. But the line dividing good and evil cuts through the heart of every human being, and who is willing to destroy a piece of his own heart?"*

-Aleksandr Solzhenitsyn (1918-2008) was a Russian novelist and Soviet dissident who heavily criticized Communism. His novel *The Gulag Archipelago* helped to raise awareness worldwide of the political repression in the Soviet Union, specifically in its Gulags (forced labor camps).

In this chapter it is my goal to have you see evidence that Covid vaccines are associated with increases in injuries and death and to introduce you to several athletes who were severely injured or died after Covid vaccination. I hope that you will question the wisdom of mandating Covid vaccines, especially in children.

I hate to say this because it's so horrifying, but the Covid vaccines are associated with death in some people and severe injuries in many people. If the powerful people who push Covid vaccination are wrong about the vaccines' safety, would they admit that to the entire world? If it's true, how will vaccinated people feel?

VAERS has captured some vaccine related injuries and deaths, but there are many injuries and deaths that go unreported. I know this because I've heard from injured people who didn't report their vaccine injuries and, as mentioned, I know of one healthy 40 year old woman who died in her sleep and her death wasn't reported to VAERS.

Again, the CDC the FDA and numerous other agencies and people in positions of power need to look into the number of people getting seriously sick or dying after Covid vaccination. People who mandate vaccines might unknowingly be causing death and injuries in their students, soldiers and workers. I don't think they would want that or could live with it in their conscience.

**A Study of 29 countries**

We will start with a study of 29 countries, and see if their rate of boosting in 2022 was associated with their increase in deaths. Igor Chudov, mathematician and business owner, did this study by downloading databases and analyzed what he was seeing. We will focus on Chudov's commentary on his numerical findings. I've read all of Chudov's articles that he has written during the Covid era, and I trust his research.

In his article ***PROVEN RELATIONSHIP: COVID Boosters and Excess Mortality in 2022 - 29 Countries Show Strong Association between "Booster Uptake" and "Excess Mortality"*** (August 30th 2022) Igor Chudov writes:

*"This article will show that there is a very strong statistically significant association between excess mortality in 2022, and uptake of COVID boosters...*

*I wanted to see if antivaxxers' hunches about the cause of excess mortality are true. So, I set out to find data about mortality in many countries and see if I can match it with vaccination or booster uptake data."*

(Chudov then shows screenshots of the databases and the math involved which I won't put here. A link to the article is in the appendix.)

Chudov goes on to say:

---

*"None of the above (analysis) would validate a statement such as "I just proved that boosters make people croak and die". That would NOT be a correct interpretation. **(hello fact checkers)**.*

*What is the proper interpretation is that there is an EXTREMELY PROMINENT RELATIONSHIP between boosters and deaths in 2022. This is an alarm signal and food for thought that needs to be analyzed further... Despite my stating clearly that I uncovered a correlation, not a causation, I personally believe that **boosters ARE a cause of increased mortality**. There are many reasons to believe this to be highly likely, but they are a topic for another article.*

**My Own Hypothesis**
*What is the underlying mechanism between excess mortality in 2022 and booster uptake?*

- *Could it be deaths immediately following vaccinations and booster shots?*

- *Could it be that boosters no longer provide "death protection", but instead increase the chance of dying from Covid?*

- *Could it be greater rates of infection of boosted people?*

- *Could it be long-term damage from repeat Covid vaccinations making people more likely to die in general?*

- *Is it possible that people keep producing "spike protein" well beyond the promised "2-3 days"?*

*My answer is: all of the above. What do you think? Any other ideas?"*

I have the same questions as Igor Chudov. Many other people do as well. It's part of our heritage as Americans to be able to think freely and ask questions.

## Injuries and deaths in athletes

Professional athletes are among the healthiest people on the planet. We don't expect them to have Covid related deaths or dying from anything; however, they have been collapsing on the field, and in many cases, dying- in alarming numbers.

Stories about the sudden deaths of athletes have been all over independent media, but I haven't seen these unusual deaths talked about openly in corporate media. I think the sudden death of athletes is newsworthy, but a news outlet sponsored by Pfizer or another corporate interest standing to gain money and power by the US response to Covid might not.

The German newspaper **Berliner Zeitung** published a report seeking answers as to why an "unusually large number of professional and amateur soccer players have collapsed recently":

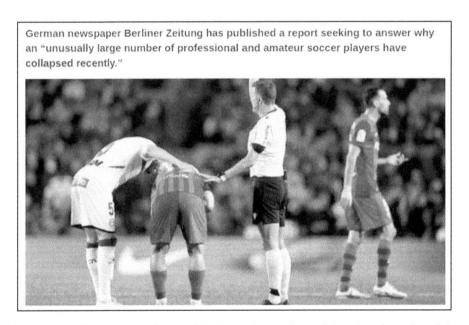

German newspaper Berliner Zeitung has published a report seeking to answer why an "unusually large number of professional and amateur soccer players have collapsed recently."

Mark Playne collects stories of injured and suddenly dead athletes. Playne is an interesting person. He worked as a writer-director and author until he saw our freedoms being stripped away and many injuries and deaths occurring in athletes after vaccination.

Playne has done a lot of Covid-related research and shares it regularly on his website **notonthebeeb.co.uk**, which stands for *not on the BBC*. He has been keeping tracks of athletes who are vaccine injured or who have died shortly after vaccination worldwide, with a primary focus on the EU and the US.

His collection of athletes' pictures and their stories is so sad to see. And while athletes have died before on the field (pre-Covid) it had been much more rare… not at all to the extent we started seeing in 2021. Again, we are talking about some of the healthiest people on the planet.

Here are some of their names and faces:

| Heart attack / Cardiac arrest | Blood clots | Deceased |
|---|---|---|
| **Preston Settles** | **Jasper Cillessen** | **Ishan White** |
| Basketball | Football | Basketball |
| Age: 15 | Age: 32 | Age: 21 |
| United States of America | Spain | United States of America |
| 14 February 2022 | 14 February 2022 | 12 February 2022 |

Why did Preston Settles (age 15) have a heart attack? Is he OK today? Can he still play basketball? Jasper Cillessen (age 32) had blood clots. Why? Can he still play football? Ishan White (age 21) died. Why did he die? All three incidents were reported from February 12th-14th 2022.

| Severe reaction - diagnosis unknown | Deceased | Deceased |
| --- | --- | --- |
| **Daniel Aakervik** | **Tom Greenway** | **Shawn Rhoden** |
| Cross-Country Skiing | Equestrian | Bodybuilding |
| Age: 17 | Age: 38 | Age: 46 |
| Norway | UK | USA |
| 11 November 2021 | 7 November 2021 | 7 November 2021 |

What was Daniel Aakervik's (age 17) severe reaction? How is he today? Why did Tom Greenway (age 38) and Shawn Rhoden (age 46) die? All three incidents were reported November 7th-11th 2021.

| Unknown | Myocarditis | Deceased |
| --- | --- | --- |
| **Helen Edwards** | **Sharad Kumar** | **Francis Perron** |
| Football | T-42 High jump, paralympics | American Football |
| Age: Unknown | Age: 29 | Age: 25 |
| Germany | India | USA |
| 20 September 2021 | 19 September 2021 | 19 September 2021 |

What happened to Helen Edwards (age unknown)? How is she today? Can she still coach football? How is Sharad Kumar (age 29) doing with myocarditis today? Can he still play sports? What caused Francis Perron's (age 25) death? All three incidence were reported on September 19th or 20th 2021.

| | | |
|---|---|---|
| Deceased | Deceased | Deceased |
| **Sebastian Eubank** | **Jen Gouveia** | **Michael Schneider** |
| Boxing | Running | Table Tennis |
| Age : 29 | Age : 38 | Age : 38 |
| United Arab Emirates | Canada | Germany |
| 12 July 2021 | 7 July 2021 | 5 July 2021 |

Why did Sebastian Eubank (age 29), Jen Gouveia (age 38) and Michael Schneider (age 38) all die from July 5th – July 12th 2021?

Are the fact checkers checking into these deaths and telling us why young healthy people are dying?

In the next chapter we learn about the mainstream media attack on Joe Rogan and Ivermectin, which should make us all concerned about the future of America.

# 19... Attacks on Joe Rogan and Ivermectin

*"The way I look at CNN now is so differently than the way I looked at CNN 15-20 years ago….I used to look at them as like, this is how I get the news. This is unbiased, professional news. They're going to tell me what's happening in Pakistan and what's happening in, you know, Mogadishu. These are the real journalists that are telling you the news. Now, I look at them, I'm like, you f\*\*\*in propagandists, like, what are you, the right arm of Pfizer?"*
- Joe Rogan (August 11th 1967-)

In this chapter my goal is to talk about the demonization of both Joe Rogan and Ivermectin. I hope that you will see the battle we are in for the truth and how hard it can be to discern the truth.

Joe Rogan is one of my favorite podcasters. He is fair-minded, intelligent and polite. He hosts **The Joe Rogan Experience** on Spotify with clips on YouTube. He discusses current events, comedy, politics, philosophy, science, sports and many other topics of interest with a wide variety of guests.

Joe Rogan has had conversations with Elon Musk, Kanye West, Neil DeGrasse Tyson, Lance Armstrong, Mike Tyson, Jack Dorsey, Dave Chapelle, Kevin Hart, Miley Cyrus, Matthew McConaughey and Edward Snowden among many others. Joe Rogan is a champion of free speech and intellectual diversity.

It's refreshing to watch people fully be able to express their points of view, question each other, disagree, maintain their civility...and laugh. Many people enjoy deep conversations and value the art of argument, which is exactly the reason that millions of people watch The Joe Rogan Experience every day.

I don't know why Joe Rogan has been so demonized by the "left", except for his unvaccinated status, his survival of a Covid infection and his opinion that trans women shouldn't compete with biological women in sports.

Here is a headline from Media Matters on December 12, 2021:

## Joe Rogan Wrapped: A year of COVID-19 misinformation, right-wing myths, and anti-trans rhetoric

Joe Rogan is not "right-wing" as many Democrats have claimed. He supported the 2016 Bernie Sanders presidential campaign and supports the legalization of marijuana nationwide. From my years of watching his podcasts, Rogan is non-partisan and issues based. He is a person with a curious mind and a gracious spirit. He treats people with good will.

He brings up topics that need to be explored. Why the sudden push for conformity on issues instead of open exploration? Isn't it worthwhile to learn why some people oppose trans women competing with biological women in sports, or why people oppose Covid vaccination? Part of having free speech rights means allowing dissenting views and engaging in debate rather than resorting to attack and demonization.

On September 1, 2021, Rogan tested positive for Covid. He began a treatment regimen including monoclonal antibodies, prednisone, azithromycin, and ivermectin. He was better within 5 days of his Covid diagnosis. Here is a screen shot of Joe Rogan as he announced that he got Covid. The top picture is how he looked according to CNN. CNN changed his skin coloring to make him look grayish yellow. The bottom picture is how he looked on Instagram:

I realize it is hard to tell the difference here. But look these images up online and you will see there is a dramatic difference.

On his decision not to get vaccinated he explained, *"I'm a healthy person, I exercise constantly, I'm always taking vitamins, I take care of myself."*

Rogan was publicly lambasted for being unvaccinated and for taking ivermectin, which mainstream media denounces as a horse medication. The truth is that Ivermectin is a medicine for animals AND for humans. It has been used successfully in people for over 30 years, and its researchers and developers received the Nobel Prize in Medicine in 2015. But proponents of the Covid narrative never tell us that.

Musical artists Joni Mitchell and Neil Young (most famous in the 1960's and 1970's) were outraged that Spotify didn't censor Rogan's views on Covid vaccines and ivermectin. Neil Young was so angry he pulled his music off Spotify for awhile. Why would artists who had once promoted freedom and peace act like that? Has the ideology of the Covid narrative burrowed itself so deeply in the minds of some people that they refuse to do research and look into things for themselves?

As sick as it may sound, it seems some people would have been gratified if Joe Rogan had died for the simple reason that he wasn't vaccinated.

**Attacks on Ivermectin**

The World Health Organization lists Ivermectin on its top 10 list of medications needed in all countries. On the WHO website we read:

*"Ivermectin is a broad spectrum anti-parasitic agent, included in WHO essential medicine list for several parasitic diseases. It is used in the treatment of onchocerciasis (river blindness), strongyloidiasis and other diseases caused by soil transmitted helminthiasis. It is also used to treat scabies."*

In some parts of India, ivermectin was handed out to people when there was a dramatic increase in Covid cases. According to the article **Unprecedented Pandemic Turnaround in Uttar Pradesh with Dramatic Decline in Cases** (May 30th 2021), the Uttar Pradesh state in India, with a population of 241 million, had reported 380 Covid cases on March 19th 2021, but by April 24th 2021, just over a month later, the number of cases skyrocketed to 37,944. As a response to the massive increase in Covid infections, and much to the chagrin of the World Health Organization, the healthcare authorities in Uttar Pradesh started an unprecedented door to door campaign to hand out ivermectin and other supplements to people in Covid kits.

Did ivermectin save lives?

**Compare India to the US**
Compare the rate of Covid-19 deaths per million between the US and India (March 2020-August 17th 2022).

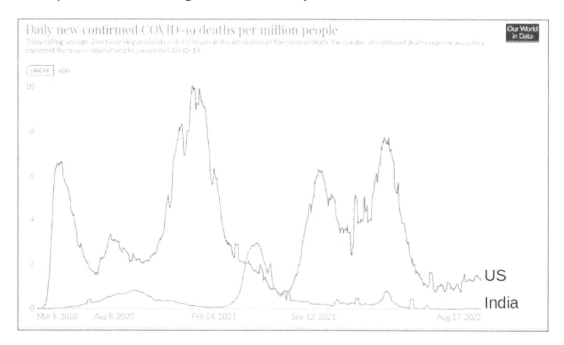

Far fewer deaths per million occurred in India than in the US.

**Compare the level of Covid vaccination** (retrieved August 29th 2022)

Approximately the same percentage of Indians are vaccinated as people in the US. As of August 28th 2022.

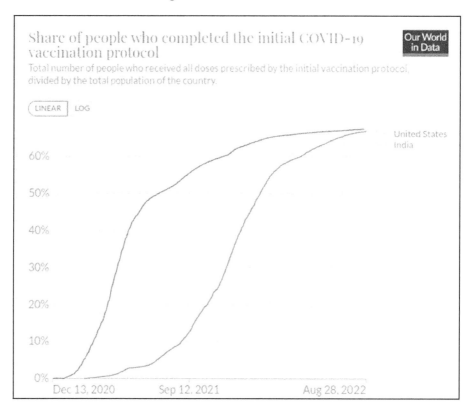

Could the widespread uptake of ivermectin in India have made the difference in their number of deaths? If it were Covid vaccines, why didn't the US have fewer deaths than India which has higher amounts of population density and poverty?

Many people in the US take ivermectin, but it is hard to get a prescription, so some people buy ivermectin sold for horses and then figure out how to make doses for themselves. Some people are also getting it shipped to them from India. We have been shown numerous studies that ivermectin doesn't work... and evidence from other studies that it does work.

Drs Kory, Marik and McCullough have successfully treated tens of thousands of people with their Covid treatment protocol, which is published on the Front Line COVID-19 Critical Care Alliance website. Here is what they say about ivermectin:

*"Since ivermectin was discovered and developed over 40 years ago, it has demonstrated an ability to make historic impacts on global health. It led to the eradication of a "pandemic" of parasitic diseases across multiple continents. These significant impacts* **earned the developers of Ivermectin the 2015 Nobel Prize in Medicine.** *More recently, profound antiviral properties have been identified. Studies show that one of ivermectin several antiviral properties is that it strongly binds to the spike protein, helping to keep the SARS-CoV2 virus from entering the cell. These effects, along with its multiple abilities to control inflammation, explain the positive trial results already reported. Ivermectin is most effective as part of a treatment protocol that includes other FDA-approved medications and supplements backed by clinical and observational evidence."*

**The changes in healthcare**

Hospitals and clinics have approved treatment protocols for Covid which doctors can't veer very far from. For example, doctors can get into trouble if they prescribe ivermectin or other non-approved Covid treatments. I've often wondered why doctors aren't sharing their opinions if they disagree with the mainstream Covid response including masking and widespread vaccination.

In the medical field, a doctor explains what is happening in the article **Why doctors aren't speaking out** (September 9th 2022):
*"You ask why doctors are silent. The electronic medical records (EMRs) are a ball and chain to physicians. We are tracked through them. When I wrote a prescription for Ivermectin for a patient, I received 5 letters threatening my medical license, my hospital privileges, and my insurance contracts...*

---

*I am almost done with my profession. I hope to retire in the next 1-3 years, decades before I had planned. I love what I do, but cannot take this toxic and broken system any longer. This is why so many have retired in the past couple years, and this trend will continue..."*

Can you imagine being a doctor with years and years of specialized training and not being allowed to care for your patient as you see fit? I feel bad for independent thinking doctors.

Should doctors be free to prescribe ivermectin and whatever they think is best for their patients?

**Russell Brand Censored by YouTube for Defending Joe Rogan**
In late September 2022, comedian Russell Brand defended Joe Rogan on this YouTube channel (which has nearly 6 million subscribers). Brand said that what he'd like to see is "open, plain communication and individual liberty and freedom to choose what course of action you want to take." In addition, Russell jokingly said the Iver word (Ivermectin). In response, YouTube issued a written "lifetime warning" claiming that Russell had violated their policies. One more joke about Ivermectin or Joe Rogan and Russell would be banned from YouTube for life,  In response, Russell announced that he was moving his popular show from YouTube to Rumble. Apparently, he is allowed to say the word Ivermectin on Rumble. Here is the link to Russell Brand's new Rumble video channel:
https://rumble.com/v1ltjqw-so-youtube-took-our-video-down.html

Joe Rogan has also moved his video channel to Rumble.
https://rumble.com/v1mqvde-former-pharmaceutical-rep-details-how-oxycontin-took-over.html

In the next chapter we will look at propaganda techniques and the discrimination against the unvaccinated.

# 20... Discrimination against the unvaccinated

*"Do not let a man who calls you 'Crazy' come too close. For if he gets you to doubt your own sanity, he has succeeded in robbing you of that which you should be most proud of: your sense of reason."*

– Martin Luther King, Jr. (1929-1968) was a Baptist minister and one of the most prominent leaders in the civil rights movement until his assassination in 1968. King advocated nonviolence and civil disobedience to gain civil rights for people of color in the United States.

In this chapter my goal is to explain several propaganda techniques which are used against us to change our thinking and behavior. My goal is also to introduce you to a few people who experienced stress due to the vaccine mandates and to show you that some countries are discouraging vaccination in younger populations. I hope that you will see how simple propaganda techniques are used to sway people's opinions and behavior.

A massive Covid vaccine campaign began in late 2020 and is still going on now in 2022, though seems less enthusiastic. Having been taught propaganda techniques by my father (Army intelligence) and having studied propaganda techniques in college, I questioned the Covid vaccine messaging I was seeing in media early on in 2020. (I do believe that Covid has been a big factor in the deaths of many people, but that is different from believing that the vaccines are the solution to preventing deaths and bringing us to herd immunity.)

Before turning to propaganda techniques, we should remind ourselves that there are two sides to propaganda: the people creating and putting out the propaganda and the people following the propaganda.

Psychologist Mattias Desmet explains how propagandists lead the population; it's like a dance:

*"Plans and visions for the future are not so much "forced" on the population. In many ways, the leaders of the masses—the so-called elite—give the people what they want. <u>When fearful, the population wants a more controlled society…</u> Those who guide the masses are not real "leaders" in the sense that they do not have the capability to determine where the masses will go. Instead they sense what people crave and they adjust their plans in that direction."*

I don't know if I agree with Dr. Desmet entirely. I think the elite do have plans for us. They basically fund the elections and once people are elected to public office, the legislation and policies they pass (or don't pass) serve the elite more than they do us. The ultimate goal in my view is we end up poorer while they end up richer and with more control. The elite have been making sure the country goes the way they want for a very long time.

A system may arise which uses our personal information like our social media behavior, what we spend our money on and our carbon usage to assign each of us a social credit score. Social credit scores determine things like your job opportunities or if you get a voice in social media. Social credit scores exist in China and may come here too if we do not recognize it and oppose it.

Basically, what happened in 2020 and 2021 is that people got scared of dying from Covid or infecting others and they trusted (corporate corrupted) leaders to tell them what to do. Hence, in 2022 we can still see some people masking their children, no end to all Covid vaccine mandates and little to no mention of the injuries and deaths associated with Covid vaccines. To question masking or Covid vaccine efficacy is akin to committing religious hearsay in the minds of some people.

**Propaganda Techniques**

Here are a few of the propaganda techniques that were employed during the Covid vaccine campaign, which served to both promote Covid vaccination and also encourage punitive and hateful postures toward the unvaccinated:

**1- Bandwagon** … urging people to become part of the in-crowd – The vaccinated were the in-crowd.

**2- Card stacking**… deliberately not telling people the whole truth – Hence, we are not being told about vaccine injuries.

**3- Plain folks**… using ordinary people to sell their product – On social media like Facebook people could attach "I got vaccinated" stickers to add to their names.

**4- Testimonial**… using famous people to sell their product- Recall watching politicians and famous people urging us to vaccinate.

**5- Glittering Generalities**…using emotional statements to sell their product – Recall the slogans surrounding vaccination.

**6- Name Calling**… using derogatory statements against people who won't use their product- We will be looking at several examples shortly. How the unvaccinated have been associated with stupidity has been astonishing.

**7- Transfer**…  dividing the population into two sides: good and bad- Recall the images of the unvaccinated as stupid.

It was because of the propaganda techniques that people believe, even in 2022, that Covid vaccines are long lasting and stop infection. It was because of the propaganda techniques that so many Americans believe that mass vaccination will end the pandemic. And it was propaganda which caused the discrimination against the unvaccinated.

Requiring proof of vaccination was not based on science. However, there was a clear line being drawn: the clean vaxxed and the unclean unvaxxed. We were living out the Transfer technique of propaganda: dividing a population into good guys and bad guys.

In Seattle, Washington the unvaccinated weren't allowed to enter restaurants, gyms or theaters for roughly 5 months from October 2021 – March 1st 2022.

One afternoon I had to wait on the sidewalk while my Japanese home stay daughter and her friends went inside the Starbucks roasting facility in Seattle and stayed inside for about 20 minutes. On the sidewalk near me was a skinny young man having, what looked like, either a drug trip or a psychotic episode. Watching him living in his different universe and wondering what his story was gave me something to focus on. However, I was still aware that some of the people entering the Starbucks were giving me dirty looks. Getting those dirty looks by several people was a little scary, more scary than the young man's behavior.

I'm close to a few young people who won't admit to their friends that they are unvaccinated. They have been ashamed of their reasonable decision. When their friends talked about getting their vaccines in 2021, these young people become experts at deflecting questions and sometimes lied and told their friends they were also vaccinated. When they were invited to "must be vaccinated" events, they lied and said they were busy.

Telling lies or playing along with a group's ideas or behaviors when you don't really feel the same way they do can have a negative impact on a person's mental health, particularly the mental health of young people.

I'm very concerned about the decline in mental health in America and in every country that has had hard lockdowns and vaccination mandates.

In Japan, unlike in the US, there are no Covid vaccine mandates and the government leaves it up to people to decide to take one after they have learned about the vaccine risks. According to the article **Japan's Vaccination Policy: No Force, No Discrimination** (December 14th 2021) we read (my underlining):

*"Japan's ministry of health is taking a sensible, ethical approach to Covid vaccines. They recently labeled the vaccines with a warning about myocarditis and other risks. They also reaffirmed their commitment to adverse event reporting to document potential side-effects.*

*Japan's ministry of health states: "Although we encourage all citizens to receive the COVID-19 vaccination, it is not compulsory or mandatory. Vaccination will be given only with the consent of the person to be vaccinated after the information provided."*

*Furthermore, they state: "Please get vaccinated of your own decision, understanding both the effectiveness in preventing infectious diseases and the risk of side effects. No vaccination will be given without consent.""*

In eastern Russia, where one of my students lives, there is no pressure to vaccinate at all (according to her), and there was no masking at her high school at anytime during 2021.

Meanwhile in the US very few people have been curious why we refused to be vaccinated. And there was little sympathy shown toward the many people who lost their jobs, and plenty of righteousness and hate, like we see in this tweet:

Guys the reality is we probably shouldnt be forcing anyone to get the vaccine but at the same time public shaming & humiliation of fucking idiots who dont get it should be widely encouraged, and businesses should be allowed to refuse service to non health reason unvaccinated ppl

12:12 a.m. · 12 Feb. 21 · Twitter for Android

There has been a lot of outright viciousness expressed toward the unvaccinated, especially in 2021.

Here is the experience of an unvaccinated man, a former computer system analyst:

**Tad Brudzinski**
@tadnewblue · 20h

I was terminated with cause in January for not taking the vaccination, despite working 100% from my home office remotely managing hospital computer systems. Not eligible for unemployment benefits despite paying into the system for over 30 years I had to retire early

32      91      303

Tad worked from home and still lost his job for refusing a Covid vaccine. He's in the same boat as millions of other people. I think people not being able to work because of refusing an experimental vaccine is newsworthy  and needs to be openly discussed, don't you?

Being 61 and having grown up in Seattle in the 1960's and 1970's I had thought Americans were different and questioned things. This is certainly a weird era for me to live through.

Another example of prejudice and discrimination comes from an unvaccinated former Seattle nurse (she was fired). In her own words:

*"I have been told by some that I don't deserve to call myself an RN… our marriage counselor "fired" us and called us racists due to our stance and 1 dentist said he hoped I'd catch Covid and die....my own national organizations will sanction me if I speak against the narrative, including taking my license away. I've picketed multiple times against the mandates and been told to f%@k off and die more times than I can count."*

Do you think people's reactions toward her vaccination status were warranted?

Also, why was this woman called a racist for refusing a Covid vaccine? What does Covid vaccination have to do with racism? First of all, she is a nurse in Seattle, which means that she probably takes pride in being non-discriminatory and leans to the left. I have been called a Trump supporter. The cancel culture crowd just throws what they think are slurs at people. One has to wonder what happened to their intellect and critical thinking skills.

One afternoon, I was at a protest opposing giving Covid vaccines to elementary school age children and was flipped off by a person driving by who also yelled out at me, "I hope you die!"

Incidentally, the Sweden, Denmark and UK have stopped vaccinating children under 12 years old due to safety concerns. Dr. Robert Malone explains in his September 7, 2022 article **The Continued Damages to our Children** (my underlining):

---

*"… the UK government is stopping the jabbing of children so abruptly that Karens across the UK are complaining that they cannot get a second dose for their unfortunate young offspring...<u>40-50% of 5-11 years of age children have a systemic reaction and between 10-15% have a "health impact" after vaccination. Not only that, about 2-4% need "medical care."</u> For a vaccine against Omicron! A mild infection in children!"*

*The CDC data … clearly shows that these vaccines are not safe for children and teens and should be discontinued immediately. The UK, Sweden, Poland and many other nations have it right. They stopped vaccinating babies and children. Parents have it right. The vast majority aren't vaccinating babies and children. It is time that the US government to face facts. It is time to stop vaccinating babies and children.*

*Beyond this - I urge parents… please think hard before you vaccine your child with these vaccines. The risks outweigh the benefits. Do not let yourself be coerced."*

We must stop vaccinating people unless they are over the age of 18 and give consent after learning about the possible risks. In Denmark, as noted earlier, Covid vaccines are not recommended to people under the age of 50. According to the **Danish Health Authority** (September 13th 2022):

*"People aged 50 years and over will be offered vaccination. People aged under 50 who are at a higher risk of becoming severely ill from Covid-19 will be offered vaccination against Covid-19. Staff in the healthcare and elderly care sector as well as in selected parts of the social services sector who have close contact with patients or citizens who are at higher risk of becoming severely ill from Covid-19 will also be offered booster vaccination against Covid-19.*

*In addition, we recommend that relatives of persons at particularly higher risk accept the offer of vaccination to protect their relatives who are at particularly higher risk."*

I love how they use the word "offer" and "recommend". Meanwhile, millions of unvaccinated people have faced discrimination. In the US our service members are even being kicked out for their refusal to take a Covid vaccine.

**Dismissing soldiers because of refusing Covid vaccination**

The US army is dismissing soldiers in the US National Guard and Reserve because of their refusal to vaccinate. <u>Is the Covid virus so much of a threat to our armed forces that we are willing to sacrifice our national security and preparedness?</u> Recall how very few Covid-related deaths occur in people under the age of 40 who are in good health. Very few. Here is an article written by Dr. Paul Alexander (August 29th 2022) explaining what's happening in the Army National Guard and Reserves.

> **US army cuts Off More Than 60K Unvaccinated Guard & Reserve Soldiers from Pay & Benefits; what a deplorable horrible act on men & women who have served & sacrificed, without any scientific basis**
>
> The Biden administration has betrayed our service men and women and with no underlying science to support this as the COVID vaccine is ineffective, failed, and unsafe & causes infection.
>
>  Dr. Paul Alexander
> Aug 29

Reading the article we learn:

*"The Army National Guard and Reserve deadline to receive the vaccine was June 30, the latest of all the services, which required vaccination last year. As of July 1, 13% of the Army Guard and 12% of the Reserve is unvaccinated. Part-time soldiers with a pending medical or religious exemption for the vaccine may continue to train with their units and collect pay and benefits. But exemption approvals are rare…. No Guard or Reserve soldiers have been approved for a religious exemption after nearly 3,000 requests. It is unclear what would qualify a soldier for a waiver on religious grounds…As of Friday, 1,148 active-duty soldiers have been removed from the Army for failing to comply with the vaccine mandate."*

Why has there been such a push to vaccinate everyone in the military? They are being vaccine injured and are one of the least likely populations at risk of death from a Covid infection.

Thousands of coast guard members are being discharged over the vaccine mandates. Meet Zack Loesch, a Coast Guard rescue swimmer who saved lives during Hurricane Ian. As of October 5th 2022, he was facing discharge despite President Biden claiming a few weeks earlier that the pandemic was over. He had filed a religious exemption but it was denied.

**So, we are willing to let go of people who could save us?**

I think that one day the dangers of Covid vaccines and the wrongness of the vaccine mandates will be agreed upon public knowledge and written about in the history books.

I also can't stand the word anti-vaxxer. It's so short-sighted, glib, pompous, dumb and above all, it shows ignorance. The Merriam Webster dictionary even has an entry for anti-vaxxer:
 *"a person who opposes the use of vaccines or regulations mandating vaccination"* (!)

Basically, if a person opposes mandating Covid vaccines, he or she is smeared as an anti-vaxxer. Call me an anti-vaxxer I guess. I imagine a sizable number of people would like to see me punished simply for writing this book.


In the next chapter we will look at some of the memes used to pressure people to vaccinate.

# 21... The Pressure to Vaccinate

*"Propaganda does not deceive people; it merely helps them to deceive themselves."*

-Eric Hoffer (1902-1983) was an American philosopher as well as a writer, dockworker and college professor He wrote ten books and was awarded the Presidential Medal of Freedom in February 1983. His first book, The True Believer, is widely recognized as a classic.

In this chapter my goal is to show you numerous examples of memes used to discriminate against the unvaccinated. I hope that you will understand how visual images can be used to sway a population.

Unvaccinated people were not as affected by the Covid vaccination campaign as the people who were eager to get vaccinated. To be sure, they saw the same programs and advertisements and images like everyone else. However, because they viewed Covid vaccines with skepticism, they were less affected by the campaign. Personally, I was impervious to the pro-vaccine messaging. To me, seeing the TV news promote Covid vaccination or people proudly share their vaccination status on social media and telling others to vaccinate was like watching a movie about another world.

However, for many months (in 2021 especially) life wasn't easy for most unvaccinated people. It was startling to see some of the memes on social media and to listen to seemingly normal people speaking so hatefully about the unvaccinated. It was open hatred.

*"Those f\*cking unvaccinated…"* *"They should be killed..."*
(I actually overheard someone say that...WOW)

When an unvaccinated person tried to explain their reasoning for deciding against taking a Covid vaccine or to share information they had learned about the vaccines, the conversation usually ended awkwardly… or angrily… or hastily. And even in October 2022, some people see nothing wrong with mandating that everyone take a Covid vaccine to get a job, enter the military or attend higher education.

I think one reason that hate against the unvaccinated spread so fast and was so virulent was because many vaccinated people believed that the vaccines would end the Covid pandemic… which they didn't and can't and won't. They also believed that unvaccinated people spread Covid while the vaccinated didn't. Simply put, some people believed false things (I'm sure a few still do) because they were subjected to repeated messaging and they were scared. Some people have been scared since March of 2020. Fear can make people do terrible things, like discriminate.

Another reason that there has been so much prejudice and discrimination expressed so openly against the unvaccinated was that powerful and influential people were showing prejudice against the unvaccinated and thus giving people the license to hate. Let's turn to a few of the images we saw in 2021 on social media.

Here's the first image, basically showing how the death of unvaccinated people is nature's way of clearing out dumb people.

The next image is used to make unvaccinated people stupid:

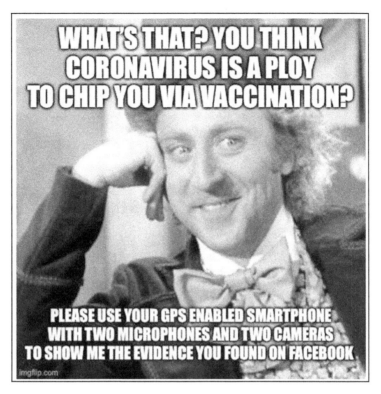

The next message is saying that the unvaccinated will take up all of the hospital resources:

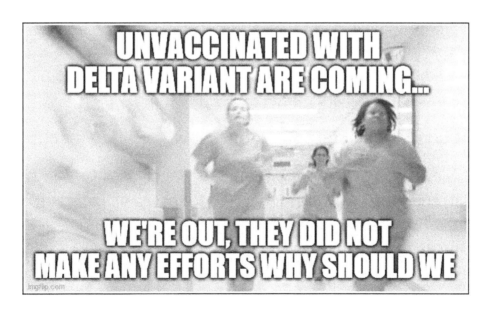

## Hospital Capacity

The truth is that very few hospitals nationwide were overwhelmed in 2020 or 2021 or in 2022. A few were for a few weeks.

However, on August 11, 2022 it was reported that Harborview hospital in Seattle, our area's trauma hospital, was reportedly at 130% capacity and non-emergency patients were being rerouted to other hospitals. From KIRO 7 news we read (my underlining):

*"Harborview Medical Center leadership says they are over 130% capacity as of Thursday afternoon. Their CEO, Sommer Kleweno Walley, says the hospital can usually hold up to 413 patients; however, 563 are being treated inside. Because of the rise in patients and lack of staff to accommodate, Walley says the hospital has decided to not take in any non-emergency patients for a moment...The reason for the increase is credited to several factors: more trauma patients coming in because of more accidents during the summer, patients putting off their treatments, etc. But Mitchell says that ultimately, <u>the pandemic has created a problem that will last for some time</u>."*

I'd like to learn details about the problems the pandemic has caused that will "last for some time" and why there weren't enough hospital workers. Did the Covid virus cause those problems, or was it our response to the Covid virus that caused those problems?

## Did Harborview lose staff due to the Covid vaccine mandate?

If Harborview were overcapacity due to unvaccinated people sick with Covid, I'm sure we'd be seeing that news blasted all over the TV news. If the hospitals were full of vaccinated people either sick with Covid or with vaccine injuries would we see that in the national news?

Let's turn to the topic of ICU beds in the US. This chart from Our World in Data shows the number of ICU beds occupied by people infected with Covid from near the start of the pandemic in 2020 through August 2022.

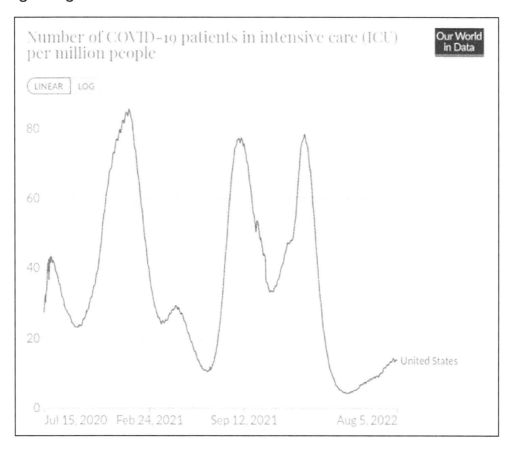

According to a March 3, 2020 article in the Washington Post, there are roughly 93,000 ICU beds in the US, which equates to 3.6 ICU beds per 10,000 people. Looking at the chart, we needed the hospital capacity to have 80 ICU beds per million people 1 time in 2020 and two times in 2021. There are enough ICU beds theoretically as there are roughly 360 beds per million people, over 4 times the number we needed for Covid infections. **The problem is that the ICU beds are not distributed equitably across the country.** Some states have more ICU bed capacity than others. Some cities barely have the ICU capacity to meet the needs of their community even without Covid.

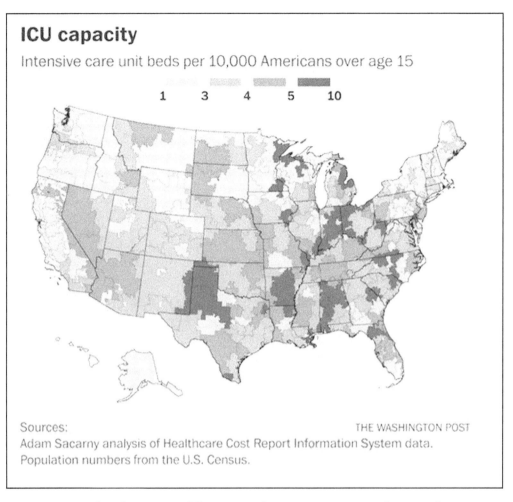

**ICU capacity**

Intensive care unit beds per 10,000 Americans over age 15

1   3   4   5   10

Sources:                                                    THE WASHINGTON POST
Adam Sacarny analysis of Healthcare Cost Report Information System data.
Population numbers from the U.S. Census.

Let's return to the images. The next image was made to trigger our fear of social exclusion if we don't get vaccinated:

The young woman is having to weigh things out: Get vaxxed, so she can get mimosas with her friends… or remain unvaxxed and stay home? This image uses the bandwagon technique of propaganda: the pressure to join a group, and the fear of exclusion.

Below is an image which convey the meaning that the unvaccinated are standing in the way of herd immunity.

Anti-vaxxers messing it up for everyone.

The image of the man peeing upstream from the clean cut guy getting a drink of water is disgusting. The message "Anti-vaxxers messing it up for everyone" is just plain wrong as evidence has shown.

Finally, we have the image of unvaccinated people as "anti-vaxxers", fat and slovenly and making life impossible for the vaccinated people, who are struggling to carry the unvaccinated to herd immunity:

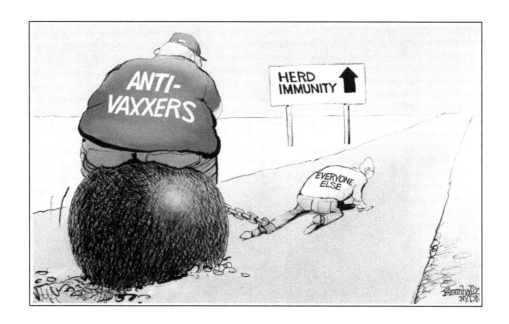

How can Covid vaccines lead us to herd immunity if they don't prevent infection or transmission? Also, in the image above, the Anti-Vaxxer's shirt is red as if he is a Republican.

How do images like this make unvaccinated people feel?

Shame? Embarrassment?

Does feeling intense shame at the age of 15, 18 or 24 impact a person's psycho-social development?

Could it lead to depression or mental illness?

Something deep and psychological is going on in our country and it's dangerous.

I made this meme in response to the prejudice and discrimination I was experiencing and sensing in society against the unvaccinated:

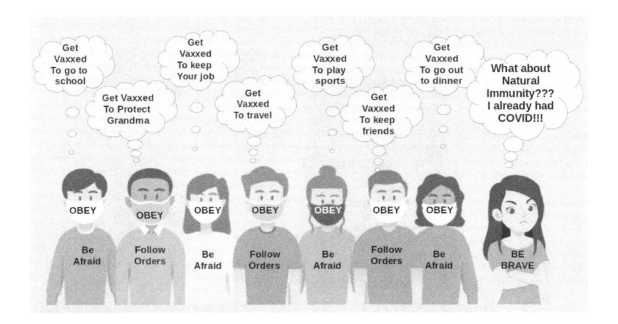

Will the unvaccinated people ever get an apology once it is common information that Covid vaccines don't protect against infection, transmission and in some cases death?

How about when it's common knowledge that the Covid vaccines are associated with injuries and death?

How about when it is common knowledge that natural immunity offers much better and longer lasting protection?

We deserve an apology.

In the next chapter we will look at how people of influence pushed Covid vaccines, including offering us incentives to vaccinate.

# 22... The Vaccine Campaign

> *"… we know that the vaccine works well enough that the virus stops with every infected person...The virus does not infect them. It cannot use a vaccinated person as a host to get more people."*

> - Rachel Maddow. (1973-) hosts the Rachel Maddow show on MSNBC. She talks about politics and aligns with the Democratic party. She has won several Emmy awards.

In this chapter my goal is to show you how people of influence and gimmicks have been used to promote vaccination. Truth was the first casualty. There is an entire industry set up to propagandize the American people. It's called marketing… and with Covid vaccines they don't appear to be done propagandizing us yet.

Aaron Ginn tweeted this to show how Maddow was pushing Covid vaccination back in March 2021:

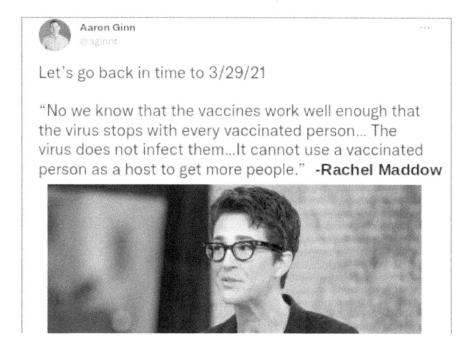

Rachel lied to her viewers. Maybe she was simply repeating what she was told to say, and she didn't know any better. However, did she have a follow-up show to apologize to her viewers and to share how she had learned they don't actually don't prevent transmission or infection?

Videos of her making those pronouncements are still on YouTube. I thought YouTube took off fake news.

Another TV celebrity pushing propaganda and divisiveness was Sunny Hosten, one of the hosts of the ABC talk show The View. On April 14th 2021 Hosten said:

*"The reason people are getting vaccinated and still need to be cautious is because of the growing number of white male Republicans that continue not to want to wear their mask or get vaccinated because they consider it some sort of freedom ride...*

*"I think people like Tucker Carlson are being very irresponsible by sending out this messaging, by sending out the message that maybe the vaccines just don't work," she said. "That is irresponsible. It's misinformation and it's causing, I think in the long run, people to die. People need to be more concerned about the virus, more scared of this virus than the vaccine."*

So… white male Republicans are inherently evil and also we need to be more scared of the virus than the vaccine? How long have we had white male Republicans in the US? Are they causing all of the problems in the nation? Why wasn't Sunny Holsten curious why so many people have been opposed to Covid vaccination and masking? And by the way, Tucker Carlson was right: vaccines don't always work.

Another person of influence promoting Covid vaccination was Stephen Colbert, who was also likely told to promote Covid vaccination. In other words, someone instructed him to propagandize his viewers. Do you remember the dancing vaccines on the Stephen Colbert Show in a segment entitled "The Vax-Scene" on June 20th 2021? Stephen made it look like taking a vaccine was a fun and that if you got one, you would be part of the cool crowd having fun too.

Finally, here's President Joe Biden on December 16th 2021:
*"We are looking at a winter of severe illness and death for the unvaccinated — for themselves, their families and the hospitals they'll soon overwhelm."*

Thankfully, Joe most all of us are still here.

A google search on top stories in January and February 2022 did not reveal any stories about the unvaccinated overwhelming hospitals or massive numbers of unvaccinated people dying.

## Incentives to Vaccinate

Aside from being persuaded by influential people to take Covid vaccines, all of us were given incentives to vaccinate, like tasty fries, donuts, a chance to win a lottery and even the promise of lap dances.

Vaccinate and get a side of fries:

Vaccinate and get tasty donuts:

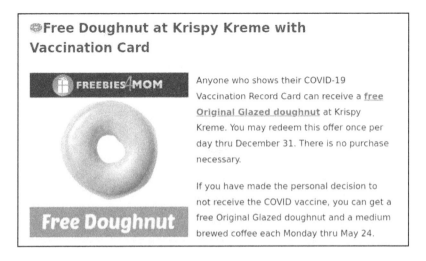

Vaccinate and get a chance to win big money:

Vaccinate so that there can be future lap dances:

Finally, on August 28th 2022 we read that the Rockefeller Foundation is still thinking about ways to persuade the unvaccinated to vaccinate! I don't understand why the people "in charge" think we are like computers to be programmed instead of human beings with volition… but of course Bill Gates is involved.

# Rockefeller Foundation Wants Behavioral Scientists To Come Up With More Convincing COVID Vaxx Narratives

 BY TYLER DURDEN

SUNDAY, AUG 28, 2022 - 01:00 PM

The **Social Science Research Council** is a non-profit group which launched **The Mercury Project** to persuade Covid vaccination.

The *Social Science Research Council* gets considerable funding from organizations, like the Rockefeller Foundation, other billionaire groups and many governments. It received a $20 million grant from the National Science Foundation.

Members of the Mercury Project are behavioral scientists whose mission is to tailor pro-vaccine messaging to specific groups of unvaccinated people. They want to figure out how to convince us to take Covid vaccines. I don't understand why the people "in power" want us all vaccinated when the data clearly shows us that death is rising despite current high levels of vaccination in most age groups. I want to know about those deaths.

If the people "in power" want to convince us to vaccinate, how about they first explain exactly what caused the HUGE number of excess deaths in 2021? Also, how about they listen to the people who have been injured by the vaccine and also from the families of people who have died shortly after vaccination? How about they ask those people what some good talking points might be to convince the unvaccinated to take a Covid vaccine?

We get to decide what we do to our bodies. "My body, my choice" isn't just a pro-choice talking point. Recall the survival rates of people of all ages who get infected. Recall the death profile and how very few people have had a Covid-related death under the age of 50.

Pushing the vaccine has itself become an industry. There are many highly educated minds, who are making a lot of money, working on propaganda techniques to convince us to vaccinate ourselves and our children.

Do you think if you were making $100's of thousands of dollars that you might become psychologically invested in keeping that money train flowing into your bank account?

Do you think you could be morally compromised by that kind of money?

Would you feel comfortable thinking of creative ways to get parents to have their babies get a Covid vaccine if it meant you got $100,000.

How about all of the money being given to the Mercury project instead be used to create more drug treatment centers, or to start a jobs program or build low income housing or give people money for food… or food itself… or create more jobs? I think we have to look at what is really happening in the US. And it's not the Covid virus.

Let's turn to the Zero Hedge article: **Rockefeller Foundation wants behavioral scientists to come up with more convincing Covid vaxx narratives**: (my underlining)

*"Mercury groups will be deployed in multiple nations and will study vaccine refusal and the medical "disinformation" that leads to it. They are operating with the intent to tailor vaccination narratives to fit different ethnic and political backgrounds, looking for the key to the gates of each cultural kingdom and convincing them to take the jab."*

From the Mercury Project's own words, we read:

*""Funded projects will provide evidence about what works–and doesn't–in specific places and for specific groups to increase Covid-19 vaccination... Each of the 12 teams will have access to findings from the other teams while exploring interventions including, but not limited to:*

*-Conducting literacy training for secondary school students in partnership with local authorities to help students identify Covid-19 vaccine misinformation.*

*-Equipping trusted messengers with communication strategies to increase Covid-19 vaccination demand.*

*-Using social networks to share tailored, community-developed messaging to increase Covid-19 vaccination demand.""*

(The Mercury program's plan is so disgusting, especially in light of the injuries Covid vaccines are causing.)

Responding to the **Mercury project** plans, author Tyler Durden says:

(My underlining and bolding)

*"In other words, their focus is propaganda, propaganda and propaganda. The very basis of the existence of the Mercury Project presupposes that individuals cannot be trusted to make up their own minds about the information they are exposed to, and that they must be molded to accept the mainstream narrative.*

*It also presupposes that mainstream or establishment information is always trustworthy and unbiased.*

***The widespread non-compliance against Covid vaccination mandates despite extensive government pressure is perhaps one of the most underappreciated events of the past century.***

*It is likely the reason why political elites and the corporate media went from a non-stop fear campaign against the public to almost no mention of Covid within a matter of weeks.*

*It was as if the populace was being put through two years of waterboarding and then one day the torture simply stopped without explanation.""*

I agree completely with Tyler's response.

We have to look squarely at what is actually occurring in the US. A kind of totalitarian fascist state with mass surveillance and overt censorship is being built to rob us of our freedom and control everything we think, do and say.

In the next chapter we will look at the phenomenon of mass formation, which explains the fervored, true-believer response to the Covid vaccines.

# 23... Mass Formation

> *"We are fast approaching the stage of the ultimate inversion: the stage where the government is free to do anything it pleases, while the citizens may act only by permission; which is the stage of the darkest periods of human history, the stage of rule by brute force."*

> -**Ayn Rand** (1905-1982) was a Russian-born American writer and philosopher. In 1957 she published her famous novel **Atlas Shrugged**. Rand rejected faith and religion and was a believer in laissez-faire Capitalism.

In this chapter my goal is to introduce you to Dr. Mattias Desmet and explore the topic of mass formation, the rise of censorship, the stages of dehumanization and the importance of allowing dissent.

Forming groups and striving to get along within a group is normal and positive. Most all of us belong to many groups. Consider the workplace. Over time, people who work together typically end up mirroring each other by agreeing on proper conduct, holding similar opinions, talking about similar topics, and even wearing similar clothing. We call it workplace culture. The same goes for friend circles. Friends typically share similar views on politics and watch the same media and talk about the same topics. Belonging to any group, there is subtle pressure and widespread agreement on what is considered appropriate speech and conduct. Groups are not dangerous if dissent is allowed and people show good will toward the dissenters. This is a very important point.

Mass formation is different from normal group formation. According to Mattias Desmet, clinical psychologist and author of the book **The Psychology of Totalitarianism** (2022):

*"Mass formation is, in essence, a kind of group hypnosis that destroys individuals' ethical self-awareness and robs them of their ability to think critically. This process is insidious in nature; populations fall prey to it unsuspectingly. To put it in the worlds of Yuval Noah Harari: most people wouldn't even notice the shift toward a totalitarian regime. We associate totalitarianism mainly with labor, concentration, and extermination camps - but those are merely the final, bewildering stages of a long process."*

There are dangers when groups demand that people behave in specific ways and believe specific things, <u>when dissent is not allowed</u>. There is danger when people going along with any narrative become unable to tolerate the people who disagree.

**That should be the rule: Allow people to disagree.**

The difference between mass formation and normal group behavior is explained in the article by Dr. Robert Malone (inventor of mRNA technology) **MASS FORMATION PSYCHOSIS or... mass hypnosis- the madness of crowds** (December 9th 2021):

(my underlines)

*"...mass formation is different from group think. There are easy ways to fix group think by just bringing in dissenting voices and making sure you give them platforms. It isn't so easy with mass formation. <u>Even when the narrative falls apart, cracks in the strategy clearly aren't solving the issue, the hypnotized crowd can't break free of the narrative.</u> This is what appears to be happening now with COVID-19. The solution for those in control of the narrative is to produce bigger and bigger lies to prop up the solution. Those being controlled by mass formation no longer are able to use reason to break free of the group narrative."*

The last sentence is the scary part:

*"Those being controlled by mass formation no longer are able to use reason to break free of the group narrative."*

I just don't know what it will take for Covid vaccine mandaters to see the error of their ways.

Mass Formation occurred in Nazi Germany. This is a picture from a 1936 Nazi rally. At the time it was mandatory for all German citizens to salute to demonstrate their allegiance to Hitler and to his vision of Germany. Yet, one man, who had been a party member, August Landmesser, was not saluting. He couldn't because he had fallen madly in love with a Jewish woman. After the Nazi party found out about their relationship, he was expelled and faced tragedy after tragedy for the rest of his life. Serious tragedies.

A person's way of thinking and reacting to things changes after they have fallen victim to mass formation, which is what happened to the German people when Hitler was in power from 1933-1945. They fell under a spell.

I have wondered how the German people were able to reconcile their thinking and behavior if they had been loyal followers of Hitler and had known of human extermination. How were they able to regain their humanity? What were the rest of their lives like?

Mass formation took hold of a huge segment of the US population in 2021 related to the "necessity" for everyone to get vaccinated. Clearly, the country was divided in 2021 and I hope that the mean-spiritness I was witnessing never repeats itself. We need to be aware of mass formation itself, so we can try to prevent it from taking hold of us.

Mass formation is nothing new either. The steer toward mass formation has been building in the US and much of the world for many years in lockstep with our advances in technology and science, and our move away from the recognition of and respect for our collective humanity.

Haven't you noticed the intolerance of different views and the increase in censorship over the last several years in the US? As if there is one right way to be in the world and about a million ways not to be. Lots of rules. In societies under the spell of mass formation, free speech is not allowed.

The White House itself seems to have called for Naomi Wolf, author of **The Bodies of Others – The new authoritarians, Covid-19 and the war against the human** (2022) and former advisor to Bill Clinton, to be permanently deplatformed from Twitter for asking questions about Covid vaccines (September 8th 2022).

She found out that the White House worked with Twitter because it was in a lawsuit's discovery documents obtained by Attorney Generals Eric Schmitt (Missouri) and Jeff Landry (Louisiana).

Dr. Wolf explains (My underlining):

*"Today my lawyers submitted a **new court filing** with additional documents that show how* <u>the executive branch of our federal government worked with Twitter to silence me for asking questions about the Covid-19 vaccines</u>*. These documents also appear to show that the censorship project between Twitter and the executive branch began inside the White House. Nobody should be retaliated against for exercising her First Amendment rights. Thank you to Missouri AG Eric Schmitt and Louisiana AG Jeff Landry for working to obtain these documents. I will continue fighting to protect my rights and the rights of all Americans to speak their minds and ask tough questions."*

Some of the most powerful people in our nation are calling for censorship. Technology can be used to end our free speech and privacy rights, the people managing the levers can simply just turn you off… by kicking you off social media platforms or by shadow banning your posts on social media or not listing your article high up on Google or you have a harder time getting a job. People with power can indirectly tell you to shut up. These overlord types forget that free speech is a fundamental American right. The reason for increases in censorship, fact checking and cancel culture is simple: powerful people want to silence voices that disagree with whatever narrative they are promoting and in this case it's the necessity of Covid vaccines for everybody.

We need more people like Naomi Wolf because speaking out is how we prevent mass formation from moving to a more dangerous stage. We are lucky in the US to have free speech rights; many countries don't. And we are lucky that nearly all Americans recognize how important free speech is.

I know how important and precious free speech is. I have taught people from many countries like Saudi Arabia, Iran, Iraq, China, Russia, and Ukraine, etc and have heard their horror stories. We don't want to lose our free speech rights. Believe me.

Wolf is an example of what has been happening to people who are stepping out of line in our society since the start of the Covid era. The reason is mass formation. A narrative was intentionally built against the unvaccinated and those who question the vaccine. I want the spell of mass formation to be broken in our country. I don't know exactly what it will take, but I do sense that it will take a rediscovering of our humanity and strength.

**The causes of mass formation**
Dr. Mattias Desmet is a professor of Clinical Psychology at Ghent University in Belgium. He started noticing the conditions being met for mass formation to occur in the US and Europe back in 2017. According to Dr. Desmet, people were primed to fall under the spell of mass formation before the arrival of the Covid virus.

A people's blind obedience to a government, (or to any leadership), can only occur after 4 specific conditions are met in the population:

1- A large number of people must feel alone and isolated

2- Their lives must feel pointless and meaningless

3- There must be high levels of free floating anxiety

4- There must be high levels of free-floating frustration and aggression

Dr. Desmet explains that after these 4 conditions are met, people are ripe to follow the dictates of a powerful group. Most everyone reading this book could come up with numerous examples of how these 4 conditions had been met prior to the arrival of Covid in the US.

That fact, coupled with the repetition of messaging resulted in many Americans becoming blindly obedient to the Covid vaccine narrative and rejecting any questioning of it. It is why many people "don't want to hear about it."

It is sad for the people who are not blindly obedient to the Covid vaccine narrative to see this allegiance in their friends, family and circle of acquaintances.

**Dr. Mattias Desmet**

Dr Desmet was in the same boat as everyone else at the start of the Covid era. He and a great many other people were reading all they could about Covid since March 2020.

Shortly after the start of Covid in 2020, Dr. Desmet, like everyone else (including me), was unsure how serious the pandemic was going to be, so he compared the actual number of deaths to the models created by Imperial College in London, one of the prime architects of the US and Europe's Covid response.

He found huge discrepancies between the projected number of deaths and the actual number of deaths. For example, it was reported by Imperial College that in Sweden, which didn't lock down or make its people wear masks, **80,000** people would die, but by May of 2020 only **6,000** people had died. Later, by November 12th 2021 15,051 had died and by August 21st 2022, **19,651** had died, a far cry from the 80,000 initially modeled 2 ½ years earlier.

Desmet was surprised that even after Imperial College's mathematical models had been proven wrong in 2020, the Covid mandates didn't change.

Also, Dr. Desmet found it curious that many countries had a unified Covid response in a very short amount of time, much of the world reacted to Covid in the same way at the same time. (I thought the same thing.) Clearly, there were orchestrating forces in place. Sweden didn't go along with the same Covid response, which is why it was singled out and demonized.

Desmet was also surprised that the majority of people went along with the government mandates with so little resistance: stay at home orders, shutting down businesses and schools, masking, postponing medical care, vaccine mandates and vaccine passports – all despite clear evidence that these policies are harmful and don't stop Covid spread.

Dr Desmet explains that about 30% of the population is very subject to mass formation. That means they likely won't back down from their pro-vaccine mandate position even if they are presented with irrefutable evidence of the vaccines' harms. 40% of people will go along with Covid narrative, like vaccine mandates..up to a point. They basically don't want to stand out from the herd. Finally, 30% of the population is not susceptible to mass formation. And about 10% of a population will speak out against things they think are wrong.

Not being able to change one's mind in light of new information is evidence of mass formation. If people who support vaccine mandates know that Covid vaccines are dangerous to many people, yet continue with Covid vaccine mandates, what kind of people are they? They are either sociopaths or they are in the grips of mass formation.

We are facing a serious situation. Many people in the US are going along with whatever people in power tell them to do. Certain politicians, public health officials, doctors and scientists, broadcasters and journalists have become almost God-like in the eyes of the public. In 2022 some people still can't admit that Covid vaccines aren't working as we had been promised in early 2021.

The essay **How many among us are suckers?** gives us the perfect example of how blindly following the dictates of the powerful can make people lose their critical thinking skills:

*"...while having lunch at a Chinese restaurant yesterday, I overheard a conversation at a nearby table between six mature and self-evidently well-educated people in which each and every one complained with great exasperation about how they had done "everything right" when it came to masks, social distancing and vaccinations and still gotten Covid.*

*But no sooner had this round-robin of complaint ended that then they began talking about the urgent need to get further boosted against the deadly plague.*

*Question the policies? Or the efficacy of the vaccines? Call into question the quality of the information they had been provided about the virus and the vaccines? Nope. Just double and triple down on more of the same. And get suckered again."*

The Covid vaccines have been marketed to us like cars are marketed to us or smart phones or wars, or the causes of the country's economic problems or the virtues of electric cars, or a million other things. And in the US every time a big event occurs or powerful people want us to believe certain things, there are always slogans that are repeated again and again, to manage our perceptions before we even have a chance to learn about the situation in detail.

We need to cognitively realize that this is happening to us. We're human beings and there is dignity in that. As human beings, we have the right to be curious about multiple sides of the stories we are told.

"You are with us or against us."

"Safe and effective"

"Stay home, save lives"

"Make America great again."

"You will own nothing and be happy."

Why do powerful people want us to believe certain narratives? It is because they have something to gain.

**The stages of dehumanization**
The Covid pandemic gave people a group to belong to… and a group to hate. In 2021 the unvaccinated were reduced to an abstraction and their humanity was set aside. Some vaccinated people then felt free to discriminate against them because the moral imperative to be respectful had been eliminated. The unvaccinated started being dehumanized. Dehumanization occurs in a totalitarian state as a way to control dissent.

There are five stages of dehumanization. These stages are important to know. Let's look at how the unvaccinated were dehumanized through the lens of the essay **Totalitarianism and the five stages of dehumanization**:

(I summarize each stage and put in unvaccinated for the target population.)

**Stage one of dehumanization of the unvaccinated was the creation and political use of fear**: fear of death. And fear of the unvaccinated was constantly being fed.

A case in point: *"That's nearly 80 million Americans not vaccinated. And in a country as large as ours, that's 25 percent minority. That 25 percent can cause a lot of damage- and they are. The unvaccinated overcrowd out hospitals, are overrunning the emergency rooms and intensive care units, leaving no room for someone with a heart attack, or pancreatitis or cancer."*

- President Joe Biden, September 9, 2021

**Stage two of dehumanization is soft exclusion**: the unvaccinated turned into scapegoats- blamed for Covid infections, and deaths and were excluded from certain parts of society. They couldn't enter restaurants, bars, gyms, theaters, etc. The act of dehumanization also includes being berated in public for being different or acting differently. (Recall how the former Seattle nurse was berated or how I was.) Here's an Australian State Premier's message, telling unvaccinated people that they can't meet with their friends and family:

*"The message is if you want to be able to have a meal with friends and welcome people in your home, you have to get vaccinated."* State Premier Gladys Berejiklian, New South Wales, Australia; Sept 27 2021.

**Stage three of dehumanization was justification for why we had to exclude the unvaccinated.** The people in power 'explain' or 'provide evidence' why the exclusion of the unvaccinated was necessary for the 'good of society' and for everybody to 'stay safe.' In general at this stage, academic research, expert opinions and scientific studies are widely disseminated through vast media coverage to promote fear and hatred of the outside group.

A quick search didn't bring up any academic or scientific articles written to strongly justify excluding the unvaccinated from restaurants, bars and gyms. I did find this article questioning vaccine passports. The author asks very good logistical and socially impactful questions.

From the article **Are Vaccine Passport a Good Idea?** (March 29th 2021)

*"A growing number of companies are signaling that they will require proof of vaccination for individuals to access their services. If an individual attempts to access a location or service and either does not have a vaccine or forgets their vaccine passport, how will it be enforced? Will there be a single system, or will each industry develop their own? What about medical privacy concerns? Will this enforcement have a negative impact on underprivileged and vaccine-hesitant individuals and communities?"*

Why weren't these questions discussed in mainstream media? The reason is that they push against the narrative and the TV news is paid to not tell us the whole truth about much of anything. Mass formation is the only explanation I can think of for the effortless roll out of vaccine passports and the unquestioning masses.

**Stage 4: The fourth step of dehumanization is hard exclusion**: the group that is now 'proven' to be the cause of society's problems and is excluded from civil society as a whole, and they lose their rights. They no longer have a voice in society because they are deemed not to be part of it anymore. (I think we will stop at step #3 because more people are speaking out.)

**Stage 5: The fifth and final step is extermination, socially or physically.** The excluded group is ejected from society, either by any participation in society being made impossible, or their banishment into camps, ghettos, prisons and medical facilities…. They have stopped being part of humanity as far as the totalitarians are concerned. (Not good.)

In our next chapter we will look at vaccine injuries.

# 24... Vaccine Injuries

*"If you actually believe that the vaxx works and have been jabbed and boosted, then why should it matter if someone else chooses not to be vaxxed. You're protected, right?"*
- Lynne Yandura (Twitter)

In this chapter my goal is to introduce you to several vaccine injured people and where you can find out about vaccine injuries. I hope that you will see that vaccine injuries are a real thing.

It's been surreal for me to see the "safe and effective" slogan repeated again and again while at the same time learning about vaccine injuries. It is easy to find out about vaccine injuries if people look. At some point injuries associated with the Covid vaccines will be undeniable to everyone including people in government agencies, mainstream media and the mandaters themselves.

There are at least 4 places where people who believe in mandating Covid vaccines could be learning about vaccine injuries.

1- People can learn about vaccine injuries by searching on social media. These examples come from Twitter:

**The Blue Room (Injured by the Vax)**
@BlueSlots · 1h

1 year ago today (my bday), I received my 2nd dose of the deadly Pfizer injection. Unaware of the side effects I went to bed and was awaken by extreme chest pains and what soon after felt like a heart attack. Many hospital visits later, months of suffering, and long lonely days..

♡ 54        ↻ 84        ♥ 270        ↥

**Tom Kay**
@TomKay05869718 · 1h
You are alive to tell your story, unlike my youngest brother who died after his 2nd vax. Hope you heal.

The Blue Room suffers from myocarditis and is unable to live normally. Being injected with Covid vaccines prevented him from living a full life. He posts regularly on Twitter. His story is very sad, and he deserves to be made whole. In response to his post, Tom Kay wrote that his brother died after his second dose of the Covid vaccine.

Here is another young man suffering from myocarditis:

In the above tweet, Its Luke wonders why people are so resistant to believing his experience. I can't imagine how he deals with people's refusal to open their eyes. I would want to shake them... or I'd end up shaking inside myself.

Next is a young man who died in his sleep. The sad news was shared on Twitter:

Irfan @IrfanFacter · Aug 27

My friend's friend (3*jabbed), 25, no pre existing conditions #DiedSuddenly yesterday August 26th. Woke up with difficulty breathing, declared dead within 3 hours in the hospital. #VaccineDeaths #vaccineinjuries #Agenda2030 #WEFcrimesAgainstHumanity

It's not normal for 25 year olds with no pre-existing conditions to die.

Here is a young woman who is vaccine injured speaking out on Twitter: *"Normally mortified by showing my face like this, however one of the many side effects of the #Pfizer jab, I will. I have NEVER had this happen to me before. My immune system is losing it! What was in it??! Why did they do this to us??!"*

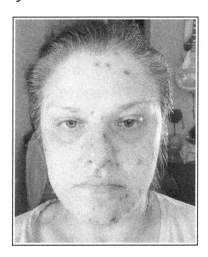

**2- On Substack,** people can learn about vaccine related injuries by listening to and reading the articles written by many highly credentialed doctors, scientists, healthcare workers in the US military and accomplished others who are speaking out on Substack and in independent media. Here are a few:

**Dr. Robert Malone** has a very widely read Substack page. He is the inventor of mRNA & DNA vaccines. In the August 2, 2022 article **Data doesn't lie: mRNA-vaccines and correlation to all-cause mortality** Dr Malone shares a transcript of a discussion he had with Dr. Theo Schetters, a virologist, immunologist and vaccine expert, highly respected in his native country, the Netherlands. Drs. Malone and Schetters discuss the timing of Covid vaccination and the timing of excess deaths to see if there is a correlation. (Marlies Dekkers is the host of the program. Both Marlies Dekkers and Dr. Shetters speak English, but it's not their native language, so their wording and grammar are a little different.)

**"Marlies Dekkers:** *So what do we now know about the side effects?*

**Dr. Schetters:** *Well, and that's the problem with this technology because this mRNA travels through your body because of the formulations that they used…. So it potentially affects all organs. And that's what the medical doctors now see, they see all sorts of symptoms that they do not know what it is. And because the adverse effects are so not just single one adverse effect, but can be anything, they surface very difficult to a statistical level. And that's why we do analysis on all cause mortality… if we do not know what is exactly related to vaccination, of course, the coagulation problems, myocarditis, we know that, but there are many more things happening. So that's why we look at all cause mortality, and in the Netherlands now it's very clear that there is a good correlation between the number of vaccinations that are given to people and the number of people that die within a week after that.*

*So let's say in this week we gave 10,000 vaccinations. Then in this week, we have something like 125 excess in death in that week ...*

**Marlies Dekkers:** *And what kind of data then you use?*

**Dr. Schetters:** *I use the data from the Central Bureau of Statistics and of our National Institute of Health. And the point is that although they report that every week, they do not report the graphs that we make. So what they do is they show the cumulative buildup of the people, the number of people that have received the vaccination, the fourth injection. So then you see a curve that goes up. You do not see the change per week, but if you calculate a change per week and you then take the figures from the Central Bureau of Statistics, where they present you the excess mortality that follows the same dynamics, the same.*

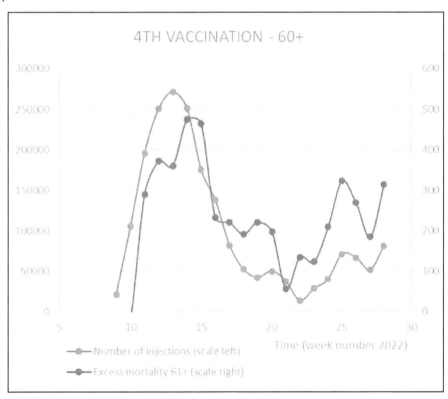

**Marlies Dekkers:** *So if you have more vaccines in that week, then you also have more excess death.*

---

**Dr. Schetters:** *Exactly. Yes.*

**Marlies Dekkers:** *If you have less vaccines in that week, you have...*

**Dr. Schetters:** Fewer deaths.

**Marlies Dekkers:** *I got goosebumps.*

**Dr. Malone:** *So all-cause mortality is the ultimate indicator for things that we didn't expect. And that's why we always have to have it in clinical research. <u>And yet once again, like so many other things, we have disregarded the learning of decades and denied the importance of all-cause mortality.</u>*

**Dr. Schetters:** *Yeah. So what we've done is we have written a registered letter to the director of our Institute of Health and presenting the results and expressing my concerns. And just with the question, from a precautionary point of view, please reconsider vaccination strategy because I think this is a real warning. And so it's not that everybody dies. Actually I do a rough calculation it's 1 in 800, but then again, but I mean, these are then especially...*

**Dr. Malone:** *1 in 800 is a pretty big number.*

**Marlies Dekkers:** *It's a pretty big number.*

**Dr. Malone:** *The myocarditis incidence now is publicly acknowledged by some governments as 1 in 5,000..."*

Do you think vaccine makers, government officials, and the people who push Covid mandates know about the correlation between high levels of vaccination and increases in deaths?

Here is another important researcher:

2. Steve Kirsch has a very widely read Substack page. His self-introduction on Substack reads:

*"….a high tech serial entrepreneur before retiring at age 64. I used to believe that the FDA, NIH, and CDC were honest organizations. I trusted them. I'm doubly-vaxed with Moderna as of March 29, 2021.*

*A month later, I started hearing stories from my friends who reported relatives who died or they themselves became permanently disabled. So I looked into it and the more I looked, the more appalled I became…"*

On July 7th 2022 Kirsch provides evidence of vaccine injuries in his article, **The safe and effective narrative is falling apart.**

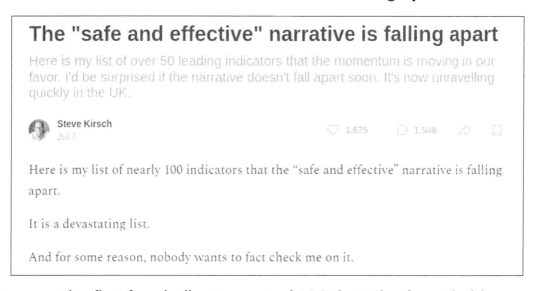

The "safe and effective" narrative is falling apart

Here is my list of over 50 leading indicators that the momentum is moving in our favor. I'd be surprised if the narrative doesn't fall apart soon. It's now unravelling quickly in the UK.

Steve Kirsch
Jul 7

♡ 1,675     💬 1,548

Here is my list of nearly 100 indicators that the "safe and effective" narrative is falling apart.

It is a devastating list.

And for some reason, nobody wants to fact check me on it.

Here are the first four indicators out of 100 that Kirsch put in his report as evidence that the safe and effective narrative is falling apart:

*" 1- Latest UK numbers shows that the unvaccinated have lower mortality for pretty much all age groups.*

*2- Turbo-cancer is being reported now. It's impossible to explain. Never been seen before.*

*3- Wayne Root reported that 33 guests at his wedding who are now sick or dead were all vaccinated. The punchline: virtually all his guests were unvaccinated. He wrote...*

*"Among my friends and family who are unvaccinated, **not one of them has died or been sick since my wedding eight months ago.**"*

*4- 4X increase in long term disability for airline pilots. The pilots union at a major US airline reported a 300 percent rise in long-term disability claims this year among its members, who are nearly all vaccinated…."*

A commenter to Kirsch's article included 34 vaccine associated injuries or deaths in her circle of friends, and acquaintances or the friends and acquaintances of her family members. Here are a few:

1. My friend's 25 year old firefighter son died within 6 hours of his 2nd Moderna shot...

2. My daughter's flight attendant friend died mid-flight from a heart attack (after the shot)

3. My brother-in-law suffered a heart attack 6 days after receiving the booster. The dr said it was the largest clot that he's ever removed in the 10 years he'd been doing this.

4. My daughter's co-workers' husbands (as in multiple) developed shingles and a-fib after receiving the shots.

5. My daughter's co-worker developed heart issues and had to wear a monitor.

People who favor vaccine mandates can have their heads in the sand for only so long. They are acting stubborn and hostile if they won't admit that vaccine injuries are occurring. Some people's bodies can't handle it.

Here is another important researcher:

## Dr. McCullough

Dr. McCullough is an internist, cardiologist, and epidemiologist. His focus since the start of the Covid pandemic has been on managing the cardiovascular complications of both Covid infections and Covid vaccinations. In a recent interview about the growing cases of heart inflammation and its connection to spike proteins we read:

*"….it is becoming increasingly evident that both the respiratory infection caused by SARS-CoV-2 corona virus and with repeated and frequent systemic administrations of COVID-19 vaccines that <u>the human body is being loaded with corona virus Spike protein.</u>*

*In the medical literature, terms such as "Spike protein disease," "Spikopathy," and "Spike prion-like illness" are appearing… the Spike protein has been found in the human heart and is believed to be the causative agent for the burgeoning epidemic of heart inflammation that has a 90% male predominance, peak incidence at ages 18-24 but can extend down to toddlers and up to men over age 65 years... We could infer that someone who has not taken the systemic exposure of Spike protein from the vaccines will be healthier and free of cardiac concerns as compared to their vaccinated counterpart."*

How can Covid vaccines be mandated?

## 4- Whistle blowers on Independent Media

Another source of information about Covid vaccine associated deaths and injuries are whistleblowers - many of which serve in the US military. Our US military takes an oath to defend the US Constitution. The armed forces are full of many courageous and honest people who signed up to defend our country from enemies foreign and domestic. Many medical workers in the armed services would feel obliged to blow the whistle if they were seeing vaccine injuries. They have integrity. I will introduce you to two of them:

1- Lt. Mark Bashaw, a preventive medicine officer in the Army reported in January 2022 that he was seeing an increase in injuries including myocarditis, pericarditis; male infertility, and tumors.

**Whistleblower: Military Covers Up Alarming COVID Vaccination Side Effects**

By Pamela Geller - on August 24, 2022

From the article **Whistleblower: Military Covers Up Alarming Covid Vaccine Side Effect** (August 24th 2022) we learn:

(My underlining)

*"In January 2022, First Lt. Mark Bashaw, a preventive medicine officer at the Army, started noticing some "alarming signals" within the defense epidemiological database.*

*The Defense Medical Epidemiology Database (DMED)... showed during the pandemic <u>a significant increase in reports of cancers, myocarditis, and pericarditis;</u> as well as some other diseases like male infertility, tumors, a lung disease caused by blood clots...*

*Specifically, the number of cancer cases among active service members in 2021 <u>nearly tripled</u> in comparison with the average number of cancer instances per year from 2016 to 2020, Bashaw said in his declaration."*

(Thank you First Lt. Bradshaw for speaking out!)

2- On August 13 2022, Greg Hunter at USA Watchdog interviewed Lt. Col. Theresa Long, Medical Doctor at Fort Rucker and one of the US Army's top Flight Surgeons. Dr. Long's job is to make sure military pilots are ready and able to fly America's complicated and lethal aircraft.

**Lt. Col. Theresa Long**

Here is a summary of their interview: (My underlining)

*"…  After months of medical observation of the devastating effects of these injections… Dr. Long, who is unvaxed, says, "<u>If you think for a moment that the very same doctors, politicians or whoever that told you this was safe and effective, if you are waiting and holding your breath for them to come back and say, oops, we made a mistake, it's dangerous and deadly, that's never going to happen.</u>*

*...What is Dr Long seeing first hand after the CV19 injections? Dr. Long says, "I have seen everything from strokes, to clots in the spleen and liver, cancers, testicular pain, infertility, miscarriages, menstrual irregularity, lung issues, thyroid dysfunction, erratic heart rates… a lot of things that I don't see in someone flying an aircraft… You can see myocarditis and pericarditis weeks and months after vaccines."*

The US Military is very familiar with the problems Lt. Col. Long has reported.  Dr. Long testified in a Senate hearing in November 2021 with doctors and medical researchers who treat CV19 vaccine injuries and patients who have experienced adverse events due to the CV19 vaccine.  Dr. Long also made a highly publicized affidavit against the Biden Administration's vax mandate as a whistleblower under the Military Whistleblower Protection Act in September of 2021.  The military brass are well aware of who Dr. Long is and the many problems she is reporting with the so-called vaccines.

What are her superiors telling her?  Dr. Long says,

*"It's always disheartening when people come to me and say privately, I completely agree with you.  I completely agree with you that we should stop these vaccinations, but publicly I will disown you.  That's not being a leader.  It's just  straight up cowardice when you know you are doing the wrong thing and you refuse to change."*

Dr. Long estimates there are

*"200,000 to 400,000 military members who are not vaccinated," and the Pentagon and Defense Secretary Lloyd Austin have threatened to kick them all out of the service.  Are the military leaders this stupid, this compromised or simply committing treason?"*

It is shocking that we may lose 100's of thousands of military members due to Covid vaccine mandates. How about we solve the problem by not mandating them? How about we opt for having a healthy and ready military defense?

**Healthcare workers speak out**
Healthcare workers are nearly all caring, moral and kind people. However, many can't speak out due to fear of job loss and many healthcare workers obligatorily follow the mainstream Covid vaccine narrative. In the article **Silenced healthcare workers speak out publicly for the first time** Steve Kirsch summarizes what silenced healthcare workers want you to know:

*"They are afraid to come out publicly (about the vaccines) due to intimidation tactics such as loss of job and/or license to practice medicine... The COVID shots are a disaster...death rates in elderly homes went up by a factor of 5 after the shots rolled out. Each time the shots are given, the deaths spike. Nobody is talking publicly about this. It's not allowed."*

*"Doctors are seeing rates of injury and death increase dramatically in all ages of people. The injuries are only happening to the vaccinated. There is no doubt that this is happening but many doctors have so much cognitive dissonance that they don't see it."*

*"One nurse with 23 years of experience says she's never heard of anyone under 20 dying from cardiac issues until the vaccines rolled out. Now she knows of around 30 deaths"*

*"I have been a nurse for 36 years. I have NEVER witnessed people in their 20s and 30s having strokes or cardiomyopathies until the Covid vaccines. I work in cardiology. When I mention that someone should look at the vaccines as a possible reason, I am immediately silenced and told, "It is NOT from the vaccine.""*

*"Doctors aren't recording vaccination status in the medical records so that all the deaths are attributed to the unvaccinated."*

*"Doctors are deliberately ignoring the possibility that the vaccines could be the cause of all the elevated events. The events are simply all unexplained."*

*"Many doctors have either quit or will quit."*

*"Some doctors and nurses at top institutions such as Mass General Hospital have falsified vaccine cards."*

*"Things don't seem to be getting any better."*

*"The medical examiners all over the world are not doing the proper tests during an autopsy to detect a vaccine-related injury. Without doing the necessary tests, it is very hard to make an association. There isn't a single "guidance" document from any medical authority anywhere in the world to do these tests on people who die within 3 months of their last COVID vaccination. This is why no associations are found: they aren't looking and it is deliberate. The mainstream press doesn't call them out on this either."* (This is an important one- If you don't look, you don't see.)

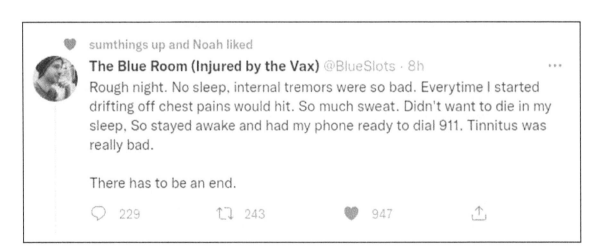

sumthings up and Noah liked

**The Blue Room (Injured by the Vax)** @BlueSlots · 8h  ···
Rough night. No sleep, internal tremors were so bad. Everytime I started drifting off chest pains would hit. So much sweat. Didn't want to die in my sleep, So stayed awake and had my phone ready to dial 911. Tinnitus was really bad.

There has to be an end.

229      243      947

## Rising Cancer Rates

From the October 21 2022 article **Cancer Rates are Increasing -- and May Get Much Worse - Wiped Out Immune Systems Take Time to Manifest** we read: *"We have a problem: cancer deaths began to increase, off the charts, in late 2021... the United States has about 800 excess cancer deaths per week... these excess deaths started just as Covid vaccination took off, and never slowed down; they are increasing and showing acceleration."*

The following chart starts in 2014 and goes to 2022. It shows the dramatic rise in Cancer deaths beginning in the first week of April 2021. There has been a steady rise in Cancer deaths ever since:

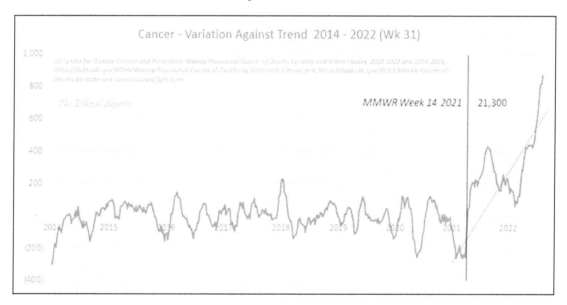

You can see that there has never been such a massive increase in cancer fatalities as there has been since April 2021. Historically, there was about 100 per week. It is now over 800 per week and continuing to rise. What happened in early 2021 to cause this dramatic rise?.

In the article **How Cancer Deaths From the COVID Jabs Are Being Hidden** by Dr. Joseph Mercola (October 18th 2022), we read these points:

#1 Analysis of U.S. Morbidity and Mortality Weekly Report (MMWR) data suggests the U.S. Centers for Disease Control and Prevention has been filtering and redesignating cancer deaths as COVID deaths since April 2021.

#2 Uncontrollable cancers the medical establishment had never seen before only started to occur after the rollout of the COVID jabs

#3 Data from the Defense Medical Epidemiology Database (DMED) showed cancer rates among military personnel and their families tripled after the rollout of the shots

#4 After the rollout of the COVID jabs in 2021, cancer patients have gotten younger, with the largest increase occurring among 30- to 50-year-olds, tumour sizes are dramatically larger, multiple tumours in multiple organs are becoming more common, and recurrence and metastasis are increasing…"

On August 20th 2022, the Ethical Skeptic published his first in a series of 3 essays: **Houston, We Have a Problem**. He started his research after the death of a friend:

*"On March 21st 2021, a longtime mentor, friend, and business partner of mine, an otherwise healthy 68 year old male, unexpectedly suffered an organ failure cascade which resulted in a shut-down of his pancreas, liver, kidneys, and finally heart. He had just received his second dose of the Pfizer vaccine on that Thursday prior. Carl quickly descended into a coma, and then died on March 26 2021."*

The Ethical Skeptic found that excess deaths for all causes (deaths above the historical average for a given week) in the US began to accelerate the same week that the administration of Covid vaccine doses peaked - the week of April 3 to April 10, 2021. (Note that these are deaths for all causes - not just cancer deaths).

As this chart shows, Covid first doses peaked at 13 million doses on April 10, 2021 and then fell rapidly. Covid second doses peaked two weeks later on April 24, 2021 at 11 million doses and then fell rapidly.

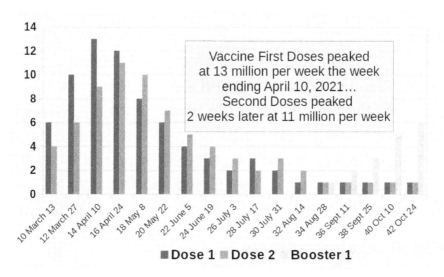

In this next chart we see that excess deaths began to skyrocket the first week in April 2021 and peaked in August 2021 - at which point the CDC began to systematically delete thousands of these excess death reports from their database every week.

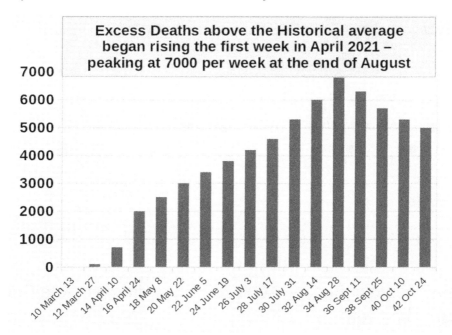

What was extremely unusual about the Excess Deaths in 2021 is that they peaked in the late summer. Historically, people die in late winter. Also, while the excess deaths went down in late 2021, they have gone up even more in 2022. Rest assured reader, many people in the US are aware of this dramatic rise in cancer deaths. What are the people at the FDA and CDC and our elected officials doing with their time? Are they blind to the injuries and the rise in cancer diagnoses and deaths? Are they morally compromised? If an English teacher such as me is unearthing reports like these from highly credentialed people and taking these concerns seriously, why aren't they? What will it take before our concerns that Covid vaccines are likely causing a huge number of injuries, including cancers, be taken seriously?

**Sudden Adult Death Syndrome**
Sudden Adult Death Syndrome- SADS sounds similar to SIDS- Sudden infant death syndrome. Here are some of the results from a search on Sudden Adult Death Syndrome (August 2022):

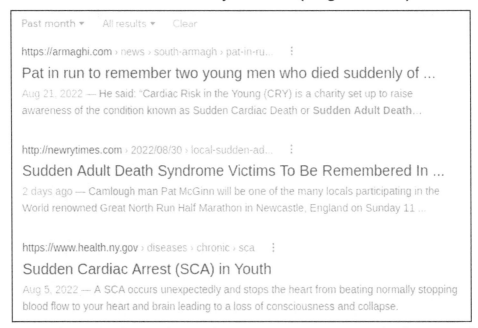

I had never heard of Sudden Adult Death Syndrome before Covid vaccination, had you?

Mark Crispin Miller, Professor of Media and Propaganda studies at NYU, reports on Sudden Adult Death Syndrome most every week on his Substack page:

**In memory of those who 'died suddenly,' in the United States, August 15-August 22**

Super Bowl champ Riddick Parker (49); celebrity hairstylist LaTisha Chong (32); seven first responders; four died after jabs mandated by their universities; two killed in "vaccidents"; & many more

Crispin-Miller shares newspaper stories of sudden deaths, particularly in young people. Here are three from the week of August 15th to August 22nd:

1- "Comstock Park High School mourns death of boys varsity basketball coach... August 16, 2022

*Comstock Park [MI] boys varsity basketball coach Tyler Edwards* **died unexpectedly** *Monday of suspected* **cardiac arrest**.*"

2) "Rising BU junior and student athlete Caitlyn Gable died at the age of 20

*Bluefield, WV - Just days before the start of the fall semester, the Bluefield University (BU) community is mourning the loss of a student athlete and rising junior.  BU announced on its Facebook page that Caitlyn Victoria Gable,* **20, died** *in her sleep on August 9. Gable was a BU Rams softball player."*

3) "16-Year-Old Dies Suddenly After Suffering Cardiac Arrest While Playing Frisbee with Family Members

August 20, 2022

*A student* **died suddenly** *on Saturday, August 6th, 2022 after suffering from* **cardiac arrest while playing frisbee** *with family members. Owen Cotty, a* **16-year-old** *junior at Methacton High School in Montgomery County, Pennsylvania* **died suddenly** *earlier this month as he was playing frisbee with his father and uncle."*

Had you heard of young healthy people dying in their sleep or dying while playing frisbee or dying from sudden heart attacks before 2021? Crispin-Miller has posted 100's if not 1,000's of these sudden deaths since the vaccine roll out. Had sudden death always existed to the degree we are seeing in 2022... but for some reason we hadn't noticed?

These unexpected and sudden deaths are now occurring nearly every day. Below is a sudden death reported on November 1, 2022 of a famous 38 year old NFL coach who died suddenly even though he was in good health and only 38 years old:

**November 1 2022 NFL Football Coach Dead at Age 38**

How many of these sudden deaths have to occur before people wake up and investigate the cause of these sudden deaths?

## #4 OpenVAERS

People can find out about vaccine injuries by looking at the VAERS database. VAERS is the vaccine adverse events reporting system – a joint venture between the CDC and the FDA. It is the place where doctors can report vaccine associated injuries and deaths. It notoriously underestimates the number of vaccine related injuries and deaths. Most deaths and injuries associated with Covid vaccines go unreported. This website OpenVAERS is a simplified presentation of the VAERS database. It is interesting (and sad) to read the reports. OpenVAERS is updated regularly.

Here is the snap shot of the Red Box Summary, which shows us the number of injuries in the US that have occurred in different categories after taking a Covid vaccine. This is through September 23rd 2022.

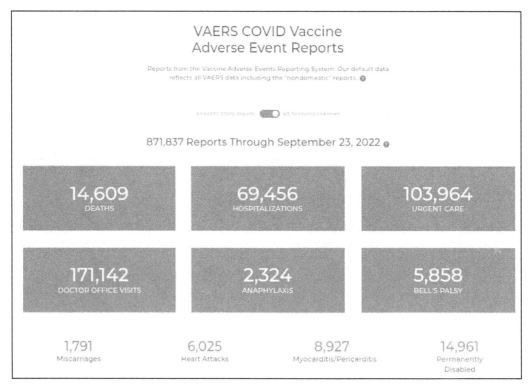

I summarize some of the injuries in this table:

**US: Deaths and Injuries associated with Covid vaccination to Sept 23 2022**

| Death | Miscarriages | Heart attacks | Myocarditis Pericarditis | Permanent Disability |
|-------|--------------|---------------|--------------------------|----------------------|
| 14,609 | 1,791 | 6,025 | 8,927 | 14,961 |

A person might look at these deaths and injuries, and knowing that approximately 224 million people are fully vaccinated in the US (according to Our World In Data, retrieved on September 10th 2022), they might claim that the chance of dying or injury is low compared to the number of Covid vaccines administered. However, we need to recognize two things:

1- Not all injuries and deaths are reported to VAERS. According to the 2009 Lazurus report: (My underlining and bolding)

*"VAERS is widely acknowledged, even by the CDC, to be vastly under reported. From their (the CDC's) Data guide:*

*"'Under reporting' is one of the main limitations of passive surveillance systems, including VAERS.* **The term, under reporting, refers to the fact that VAERS receives reports for only a small fraction of actual adverse events..***"*

The Lazarus report from Harvard Pilgrim Health Care in 2009 used Epic (one of the largest electronic medical records systems used in the US) to gather data automatically from the system...

*"Adverse events from drugs and vaccines are common, but under reported...fewer than 1% of vaccine adverse events are reported."*

*The results clearly showed that injury was much more common than the one-in-a-million lie that is often cited."*

2- We don't know if people who have taken Covid vaccines will suffer serious health problems in the future. Will doctors be able and willing to consider connecting a fast moving cancer in an otherwise healthy young person to Covid vaccination? Even if they do, the cancer-stricken person will have no recourse. Neither do the many people who are suffering from vaccine injuries.

There are vaccine mandates; however, vaccine manufacturers themselves are not liable for vaccine injuries.

In a Newsweek article **Fact Check: Are Pharmaceutical Companies Immune From COVID-19 Vaccine Lawsuits?** (January 21st 2021): (My underlining)

*"According to 42 U.S. Code § 300aa–22, <u>"No vaccine manufacturer shall be liable in a civil action for damages arising from a vaccine-related injury or death associated with the administration of a vaccine after October 1, 1988,</u> if the injury or death resulted from side effects that were unavoidable even though the vaccine was properly prepared and was accompanied by proper directions and warnings."*

*In other words, companies that manufacture vaccines are not liable if someone has an allergic reaction or injury after being vaccinated. However, individuals can file a petition with the National Vaccine Injury Compensation Program (VICP) administered by the U.S. Department of Health and Human Services (HHS) to receive compensation if they are found to have been injured by one of the vaccines covered by VICP… Though VICP covers vaccines for diseases including human papillomavirus (HPV), measles, mumps, polio and seasonal influenza, it does not cover any COVID-19 vaccines."*

Pretty shocking, right?


In the next chapter we will look at how the mainstream is awakening.

# 25... The Mainstream is Awakening

*"In highly vaccinated nations around the world, births are down significantly and excess mortality is up significantly... It is time to give the depopulation 'conspiracy theorists' an apology."*

- Chris Waldburger, Writer in South Africa

In this chapter my goal is to share how the conspiracy theorists seem to be correct about Covid vaccines causing a decrease in birth rates, and also to introduce two reports from mainstream sources: 1 from Politico and the other a mainstream academic study. Here's to the awakening!

I read Waldburger's article **Has the depopulation hypothesis been proven correct?** (September 15th 2022) in which he wrote about the connection between high rates of vaccination and increases in deaths from non-Covid causes in 2021 and 2022:

*"Science is about forming hypotheses and testing them. Well, the vaccine hypothesis was that mandating it and sticking needles into all arms available would finally bring down excess mortality, and that there would be no possible side effects like infertility, because vaccines are always super-safe. Plus we had flattened the curve with masks and lockdowns thus saving our hospitals.*

*The paranoid hypothesis was that corporations and the government hate you, they have never cared about your health before…*

*Israel, Germany, Australia, Switzerland, just as some examples, are all showing mortality levels at significant excess. All forced vaccinations on their citizens."*

Waldburger then shows us several charts to prove his point like this one from Australia:

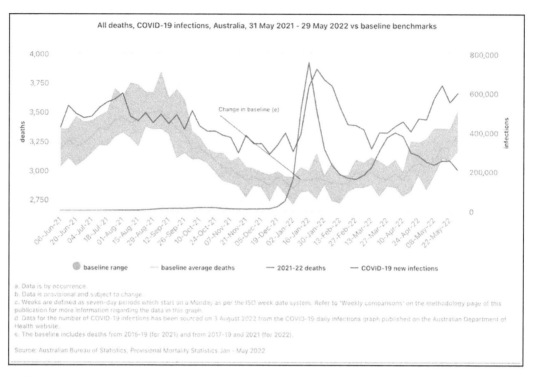

Waldburger shares an analysis of the death trend in Australia in 2021 and 2022 by another journalist who goes by the name *Trust the Evidence:*

*"From June 2021 to May 2022, there were 16,467 more deaths than normal in Australia; 5,619 of these were attributed to Covid, and 10,848 were not explained and weren't Covid."*

Just like the US, right? We are seeing a trend of much higher levels of deaths not caused by the Covid virus in countries worldwide and the increases in death are being noticed and analyzed by many people. The only common factor these increases worldwide can be attributed to is our response to Covid (masks and lockdowns) and mass Covid vaccination. Even suggesting that Covid vaccines could be a contributing factor in these deaths is taboo in the US… for now. However, in other countries the news is coming out.

Here is a May 31st 2022 headline from **Israel National News:**

> ## New study links COVID vaccines to 25% increase in cardiac arrest for both males & females
>
> **Study based on data from emergency services. COVID infection itself not linked to significant increase in cardiovascular complications.**
>
>  Y Rabinovitz / May 31, 2022, 4:20 PM (GMT+3)

Powerful forces have been behind our collective Covid response in the US as well as the push to vaccinate the entire population. Powerful forces are equally behind what information we are allowed to see and think about in the US. One of those forces is Bill Gates. Gates along with his billionaire friends don't seem to want the American public to be aware of things like excess deaths and vaccine injuries, but we may be starting to see mainstream media report these things. It is good news that the truth is coming out.

Politico is considered to be mainstream media. A Politico article was published (September 14th 2022) with initially a very long title: **How Bill Gates and his partners took over the global Covid response -** *Four health organizations, working closely together, spent almost $10 billion on responding to Covid across the world. But they lacked the scrutiny of governments, and fell short of their own goals, a POLITICO and WELT investigation found.*

In the Politico article we read this very important question posed by the vaccine policy advisor at **Doctors without Borders:**

*""What makes Bill Gates qualified to be giving advice and advising the US government on where they should be putting the tremendous resources?" asked Kate Elder, senior vaccines policy adviser for the Doctors Without Borders' Access Campaign."*

Shortly after publishing the article, Politico changed its original title to **How four powerful groups used their clout to control the global Covid response- with little oversight.**

I guess Mr. Gates is above reproach.

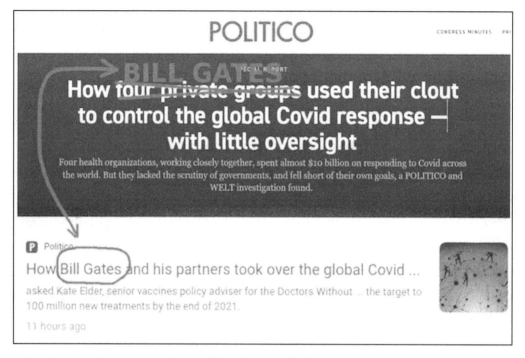

The six key takeaways found in the article are:

1 The four organizations have spent almost $10 billion on Covid since 2020 – the same amount as the leading US agency tasked with fighting Covid abroad.

2 The organizations collectively gave $1.4 billion to the World Health Organization, where they helped create an initiative to distribute Covid-19 tools. That program failed to achieve its benchmarks.

3 The organizations' leaders had unprecedented access to the highest levels of governments, spending at least $8.3 million to lobby lawmakers and officials in the US and Europe.

---

4 Officials from the US, EU and representatives from the WHO rotated through these four organizations as employees, helping them solidify their political and financial connections in Washington and Brussels.

5 The leaders of the four organizations pledged to bridge the equity gap. However, during the worst waves of the pandemic, low-income countries were left without life-saving vaccines. (Note: I question if the vaccines were life-saving at all except for maybe in the two oldest age groups 75-84 and 85+)

6 Leaders of three of the four organizations maintained that lifting intellectual property protections was not needed to increase vaccine supplies – which activists believed would have helped save lives...

The Politico article also includes a quote by Georgetown University professor Lawrence Gostin:

*""Putting it in a very crass way, money buys influence. And this is the worst kind of influence. Not just because it's money […] but also, because it's preferential access, behind closed doors."*

- Lawrence Gostin, Georgetown University professor who specializes in public-health law

Igor Chudov wrote about the Politico article in his article **POLITICO: How Bill Gates Took Over the Covid Pandemic -** Gates took over Covid just like he took over Operating Systems (September 15 2022)

*"Shortly after publishing their article with the aforementioned title, Politico changed its title to* **How four powerful groups took over the global Covid response***. In it they describe how the pandemic response was taken over by the Bill and Melinda Gates Foundation, GAVI, CEPI, and the Wellcome Trust. All four organizations pretend to be independent, but* **all were financed by Bill Gates.**

*Nevertheless, the mere publication of this article has huge importance. The things that most of us know and talk about, are appearing in the so-called "mainstream press" — after the damage was all done, of course.*

***The virus was released; millions died; over a billion young people were force-vaccinated under false pretenses***. *When it is too late to change anything, Politico is finally stating the obvious. Still, it is better than nothing. Almost everything in the Politico article was known a year ago. Where was Politico then? Busy taking government Covid vaccine advertising money.* ***The pandemic was a crime, not an accident."***

I understand Chudov's sentiment about Politico being late to the game, but what publishing that article meant to me is that the truth can only be hidden for so long. It's bound to come out, even in mainstream media.

It is also satisfying to see doctors changing their opinions on Covid vaccination. Dr. Michael Turner changed his mind about Covid vaccines. In his essay **Losing My (Vaccine) Religion: A Doctor's Journey From Hope to Despair - A Tragic COVID Opera in 4 Acts**, Dr Turner chronicles his journey from being a Covid vaccine enthusiast to being a Covid vaccine questioner. He talks about the vaccine injuries he has seen:

*"...let's talk about real, individual people. Like my family.  Like my 23-year-old daughter (healthy nursing student) who, after her mandatory vaccine, complains of persistent difficulty with concentration and memory. Or my 17-year-old daughter's friend -- last year a district-champion long-distance runner, this year struggling to complete workouts due to persistent chest pain."*

Toward the end of his essay Dr. Turner writes about the coercion happening in the medical field as well as vaccine mandates:

*"My doctor friend, employed by our local hospital, offers this confessional: "We received an email stating if we brought up concerns about the vaccine or were less than enthusiastic about encouraging each patient to get it, we would be subject to termination."*

He is a pediatrician.

Meanwhile, back on the farm, in a strident appeal published in the British Medical Journal, a group of doctors cogently lay out a case against vaccine mandates, and as regards children, end by saying:

*"For young age groups, in whom Covid-related morbidity and mortality is low, and for those who have had Covid-19 infection already, and appear to have longstanding immunological memory, the harms of taking a vaccine are almost certain to outweigh the benefits to the individual, and the goal of reducing transmission to other people at higher risk has not been demonstrated securely."*

I think it best if we listen to doctors who put their careers and reputation on the line. Thank you Dr. Turner! History will remember you well.

In addition to the Politico article, Reuters published an article on October 12th 2022 entitled **New data is out on COVID vaccine injury claims. What's to make of it?**

In the article they describe the CDC's response to a Freedom of Information Act asking for its data on vaccine side effects. The FOIA request was made by the Informed Consent Action Network, or ICAN, a Texas-based nonprofit that opposes "medical coercion" in favor of individual healthcare choices. In response to the FOIA request, the CDC had promised to give a full account of the side-effects it had collected from about 10 million people who had signed up for its "v-safe" program, a smartphone-based system that monitors side effects from the Pfizer, Moderna and Johnson & Johnson COVID-19 vaccines. The CDC had promised to post all side effects it had gathered on its website on or before September 30ᵗʰ 2022 but missed that deadline.

While the CDC has not published the injuries (side effects) on its website, it did hand over the v-safe data (minus personal identifying information) to the Informed Consent Action Network. The information the CDC handed over was astonishing.

From the article we read: (my underlining)

*ICAN (The Informed Consent Action Network) crunched the (CDC) numbers on its own and came up with some statistics that its lawyer says appear to be "alarming."*

*According to ICAN, <u>7.7% of the v-safe users -- 782,913 people</u> -- reported seeking medical attention via a telehealth appointment, urgent care clinic, emergency room intervention or hospitalization following a COVID-19 vaccine.*

*<u>About 25%</u> of v-safe users said they experienced symptoms that required them to miss school or work or prevented them from doing other normal activities...*

*ICAN counsel Aaron Siri of Siri & Glimstad, who led the FOIA litigation against the agency, said that because some vaccine-related adverse effects (chronic arthritis, thrombocytopenia, Guillain-Barré syndrome, myocarditis and more) can appear weeks after vaccination, it's important to broaden the time frame beyond the one-week window in research the CDC cited.*

*"<u>This is a large and concerning number of negative health impacts</u>," Siri said of ICAN's conclusions, adding that he's aware of no comparable public data for other vaccines."*

**What we are actually facing is a massive amount of corruption and collusion on a grand scale.**

When we allow billionaire money to rule politics and policies and the media message, and speech to be canceled, we aren't living in a Democracy. We are living in an entirely different system, one in which we are being herded to pledge allegiance to whatever narrative the billionaire class throws our way. Again, I believe we are headed toward living under a technological control grid with social credit scores, like China has wherein people are allowed privileges based on their behavior… and I hope I'm wrong.

Finally, going full circle back to my thesis that Covid vaccines should not be mandated to enter higher ed, the military or the workplace, we read this study conducted by academics, doctors and scientists associated with top universities in the US:

**COVID-19 Vaccine Boosters for Young Adults: A Risk-Benefit Assessment and Five Ethical Arguments against Mandates at Universities**

50 Pages Posted: 12 Sep 2022

Kevin Bardosh - University of Washington; University of Edinburgh - Edinburgh Medical School

Alison Krug - Artemis Biomedical Communications LLC

Euzebiusz Jamrozik - University of Oxford

Trudo Lemmens - University of Toronto - Faculty of Law

Salmaan Keshavjee - Harvard University - Harvard Medical School

Vinay Prasad - University of California, San Francisco (UCSF)

Martin A. Makary - Johns Hopkins University - Department of Surgery

---

Stefan Baral - John Hopkins University

Tracy Beth Hoeg - Florida Department of Health; Sierra Nevada Memorial Hospital

The abstract, in part, reads (my bolding):

*"Students at North American universities risk disenrollment due to third dose COVID-19 vaccine mandates. We present a risk-benefit assessment of boosters in this age group and **provide five ethical arguments against mandates...**University booster mandates are unethical because:*

*1) no formal risk-benefit assessment exists for this age group;*

*2) vaccine mandates may result in a net expected harm to individual young people;*

*3) mandates are not proportionate: **expected harms are not outweighed by public health benefits given the modest and transient effectiveness of vaccines against transmission;***

*4) US mandates violate the reciprocity principle because rare serious vaccine-related harms will not be reliably compensated due to gaps in current vaccine injury schemes; and*

*5) mandates create wider social harms. We consider counter-arguments such as a desire for socialization and safety and show that **such arguments lack scientific and/or ethical support...**"*

I encourage you to read the study in its 50 page entirety. Reading their report, I have hope that vaccine mandates will end.


Finally, the next chapter is our conclusion.

# Conclusion... Hope for the future and final thoughts

Thank you for reading this book. I felt I had to write it. The Covid vaccine should not be mandated for any reason, not to have a job, not to go to school, not to play sports or enter a restaurant, gym, movie theater, or attend a social event. The decision to take a Covid vaccine should be made in a private conversation between a doctor and a patient. The risks and benefits should be weighed. Part of that consultation should be on how to improve the patient's immune system to decrease his or her chance of getting a Covid infection.

It is a reasonable decision to refuse a Covid vaccine. There should be no stigma against being unvaccinated. Beyond that, there is evidence that the Covid vaccine are decreasing people's immune systems, leading to increases in cancer and auto-immune diseases and leading to deaths in people we wouldn't expect to die.

We learn from others and have a God-given right to express ourselves. It's why free speech is so important. My dad taught me to be wary when dissent isn't allowed. As talked about in the chapter on Mass Formation, when we don't allow speech, we are likely ushering in a system of top-down control.

I have read the writing of Toby Rogers during the Covid era. He sums up the Covid vaccine situation well:

"• The shots have negative efficacy and the worst side effect profile ever seen. Quintuple-dosed bougiecrats look like sh*te and are dropping dead left and right yet still don't understand what is happening to them (nor do they want to understand).

• The mainstream media has lied to us every single day for the last three years. At this point they are incapable of telling the truth because their business model depends on promoting profitable lies.

• Universities and schools require young people in their care to be injected with a product that is known to cause myocarditis even though this population is not at significant risk…"

Clearly, the results of "Safe and Effective" Covid vaccination aren't what most people had expected.

The situation we find ourselves in is VERY concerning.  You can read about this very depressing assault on our 4th Amendment- our right to privacy in the article **Millions of Americans Were Assigned 'COVID-19 Violation' Scores Based on Cellphone Data Collected During Lockdowns**.

Essentially, we are spied on and ranked according to our vaccination status and attitude toward Covid vaccination:

*"A voter analytics firm harvested data from millions of Americans' cellphones during the 2020 COVID-19 lockdowns and used the data to assign phone users a "COVID-19 decree violation" score and a "COVID-19 concern" score, according to a whitepaper released by PredictWise, the firm that harvested the data."*

PredictWise was able to spy on people via their smart phones to see how often they left their homes during the lockdown. If a person went out a lot they got a high score on Covid-19 decree violations while those who stayed home scored low on Covid-19 violations. PredictWise gave that information to people running for office as well as to vaccine marketers, so they could customize vaccine messaging. They use your smart phones against you. (I don't have one.)

PredictWise claims it "tracks the opinions, attitudes, and behaviors" of more than 260 million Americans, which are likely the number of smart phones owned by adults in the US.

According to Predictwise, their spying helped at least one U.S. Senate campaign:

*"… the Arizona Dems Coordinated Campaign…. was able to deploy this real-time location model to open up just over 40,000 persuasion targets that normally would have fallen off, allowing them to give the right message to the right voter at the right time."*

Unbelievable. My parents and grandparents are rolling in their graves...as are the parents and grandparents of most Americans. Clearly this is an example of technology being used for evil.

We get to decide on the country we want.

Incidentally, PredictWise was founded in 2017 by former Microsoft and Facebook employees: Tobi Kontizer (Facebook) and David Rothschild (Microsoft).

In the case of Covid vaccine mandates I believe justice will prevail as it did in this case:

And finally, I leave you with Dr. Aseem Malhotra's awakening.  Dr. Malhotra's father had been in excellent health, but then died a few months after Covid vaccination. His father's death led Dr. Malhotra to do research into Covid vaccines. Here is what he has to say:

*"There is a strong scientific, ethical and moral case to be made that the current COVID vaccine administration must stop until all the raw data has been subjected to fully independent scrutiny. Looking to the future the medical and public health professions must recognize these failings and eschew the tainted dollar of the medical-industrial complex. It will take a lot of time and effort to rebuild trust in these institutions, but the health – of both humanity and the medical profession – depends on it."*

- Dr. Aseem Malhotra September 26th 2022

Dr. Aseem Malhotra. (Courtesy of Dr. Aseem Malhotra)

PREMIUM   VACCINES & SAFETY

Doctor Turns Against Messenger RNA COVID-19 Vaccines, Calls for Global Pause

By Zachary Stieber and Jan Jekielek      September 26, 2022   Updated: September 26, 202A A   🖶 Print

I feel we are dealing with evil. I feel like we are in a war against very powerful people who are willing to risk our lives in order to increase their short term profits.  But I also believe that in the end good will prevail. It has to.

# Appendix

Here are some people who have regularly published information on Substack about risks related to Covid vaccines as well as other Covid related news:

Dr. Vinay Prasad

Eugyppius: a plague chronicle

Mark Crispin Miller

Dr. Robert Malone

Midwestern Doctor

Steven Kirsch

Mathew Crawford

Dr. Paul Alexander

Dr. Pierre Cory

CJ Hopkins

Igor Chudov

Dr. Meryl Nass

Dr. Remnant

Rounding the earth newsletter (Mathew Crawford)

Utobian (Toby Rogers)

John Dee

The Rowen Report, Dr. Robert Jay Rowen

Naomi Wolf

James Lyons-Weiler,

Bad Cattitude

Chris Waldburger

Dr. Byram W. Bridle

Jordon Schactel

Mattias Desmet

Tessa Lena

**YouTube Channels**

Mattias Desmet

Dark horse podcast: Heather Heying, Bret Weinstein

Kim Iversen

Jimmy Dore

Dr. John Campbell

Neil Oliver

**Rumble Video Channels**

Joe Rogan

Russell Brand

**Websites**

The Brownstone Institute

https://brownstone.org/

Geert Vanden Bossche

https://www.voiceforscienceandsolidarity.org/

Dr Peter McCullough

https://www.petermcculloughmd.com/

Dr. Ryan Cole

https://totalityofevidence.com/dr-ryan-cole/

The Great Barrington Declaration

https://gbdeclaration.org/

Greg Hunter

USAWatchDog.com

Dr. Pierre Cory

https://drpierrekory.com/

Robert F. Kennedy, Jr.

https://childrenshealthdefense.org/defender/

Open VAERS

https://www.openvaers.com/

Totality of Evidence

https://totalityofevidence.com/

Doctors for Covid ethics

https://doctors4covidethics.org/

We Forum https://www.weforum.org/

**Sources Cited** (Nearly all information can be found on the internet.)

**Chapter 1- Comparing the deaths in 2020 and 2021**

CDC vaccine tracker

https://data.cdc.gov/Vaccinations/COVID-19-Vaccination-and-Case-Trends-by-Age-Group-/gxj9-t96f

**Chapter 2- Covid deaths in Canada in the summer of 2022**

Government of Canada; COVID-19 epidemiology update; September 16th 2022 (Updated on September 23rd); https://health-infobase.canada.ca/covid-19/archive/2022-09-16/index.html

Government of Canada; COVID-19 epidemiology update; July 1st 2022 (Updated on July 4th)

https://health-infobase.canada.ca/covid-19/archive/2022-07-01/index.html

(To find the same charts I put in the book: Go to Figure 5 and change the option from Distribution to Number. Then click Text Description.)

Washington State Department of Health; Covid-19 dashboard; Disease activity and testing  (Click on total counts, statewide, deaths)

https://doh.wa.gov/emergencies/covid-19/data-dashboard#tables

City News; Youtube; May 27th 2021; Toronto woman develops Bell's palsy after COVID vaccine

**Chapter 3 – Our shared history**

Yelp Local Impact Report; September 2020

White, Nicolette; Burlington County Times; August 15th 2022; South Jersey Black small business owners don't sugarcoat negative impacts of COVID

McDonald, Kerry; Fee Times; December 11th 2022; Cambridge Study: Children's Mental Health Deteriorated 'Substantially' During Lockdown

Real Clear Politics; RCP Corona virus tracker; Corona virus (COVID-19) Global Deaths

## Chapter 4- The road less traveled

Oaklander, Mandy; Time; April 22, 2020; Almost Every Hospitalized Corona virus Patient Has Another Underlying Health Issue, According to a Study of New York Patients

UC Davis Health; February 15th 2022; What is the link between vitamin D levels and COVID-19?

OpenVAERS(.)com; Click on "search reports", and look to the left and fill out the fields. Also click on "Covid vaccine data" and then "Red box summaries".

Koka, Anish MD; Substack; August 10th, 2022; Vaccine myocarditis update from Thailand

Fraser, Terrence; AP news; November 11th 2020; Social media posts misrepresent myocarditis risk

## Chapter 5- Seven reasons people chose not to get a Covid vaccine

Washington State Department of Health; August 10th 2022; SARS-CoV-2 Vaccine Breakthrough Surveillance and Case Information Resource

Chudov, Igor; Substack; April 27th 2022; mRNA Vaccine Skeptics are the True Critical Thinkers

Glennon, Mark; Wirepoints; September 27th 2020;  New CDC Estimates: Fatality Rate For COVID-19 Drops Again And May Surprise You – Wirepoints

Rahhal, Natalie; Dailymail; December 4th 2020; Pfizer CEO not certain Pfizer CEO admits he is 'not certain' their COVID-19 shot will prevent vaccinated people from spreading the virus - as the firm cuts the number of doses it will ship this year

Schachtel, Jordan; Substack; October 26th 2022; Event 201: organizers of WEF-Gates pre-Covid simulation warned of 'similar pandemic in the future' - A smoking gun?

A Midwestern Doctor; Substack; October 20th 2022; Who Owns the CDC

World Economic Forum; Partners

https://www.weforum.org/partners#search

Center for Health and Security; Event 201

https://www.centerforhealthsecurity.org/our-work/exercises/event201/

John Hopkins Cary business school; Symposium featuring Fauci explores future of vaccine and virus; November 23rd 2020

## Chapter 6- Covid Vaccination rates and an example of a vaccine exemption form

CDC (data.cdc.gov); Vaccines, Covid-19; Vaccination and Case Trends by Age Group

Tieu, Van; ABC10; July 30th 2020; VERIFY: Do hospitals get more funding by marking deaths COVID-19 related?

KIRO 7 News Staff; My Northwest; October 5, 2022; Experts warn of King County COVID surge, few people have gotten updated booster

## Chapter 7- Corona viruses and the difficulty in making a Covid vaccine

Khan, Jo; ABC Health and Wellbeing; April 16th 2020;  We've never made a successful vaccine for a corona virus before.

Yeardon, Michael; Doctors for Covid Ethics; April 10th 2022; The Covid lies (report)

Healy, Melissa; LA Times; November 4th 2021; Study shows dramatic decline in effectiveness in all three Covid -19 vaccines over time

Malone, Robert; Substack; August 2nd 2022; Data doesn't lie: mRNA-vaccines and correlation to all-cause mortality

## Chapter 8- Covid Vaccine Efficacy

Alexander, Paul; Brownstone Institute; October 28th 2021; 53 studies on vaccine efficacy (Note: previously 16 studies at time of reading)

Link to 2022 California Moderna Study

https://www.medrxiv.org/content/10.1101/2022.09.30.22280573v1

Craymer, Lucy; Reuters; July 22nd 2022; New Zealand Covid death rate at record levels

Tseng, Hung Fu et al., medRxiv; September 30, 2022; Effectiveness of mRNA-1273 against infection and COVID-19 hospitalization

Xu Yiyi, Li Huiqi; The Lancet; September 20, 2022;  Effectiveness of COVID-19 Vaccines Over 13 Months Covering the Period of the Emergence of the Omicron Variant in the Swedish Population

New Zealand Covid data

https://www.health.govt.nz/covid-19-novel-coronavirus/covid-19-data-and-statistics/covid-19-vaccine-data#total-vaccinations

## Chapter 9- How do mRNA vaccines work?

Spike Protein Detox Guide; World Council For Health; Resources; November 30th 2021

US Food and Drug Administration (FDA.gov); Emergency Use Authorization

CDC, Understanding how mRNA vaccines work

Byram, Brindle Dr; Substack; September 18th 2022; Moderna's CMO Believes Spikes from the mRNA Vaccine Get to the Heart

Dr. Remnant;  Substack; February 6th 2022; First Principles | The Problem with Gene-based Injections - Part 1

Polykretis, P; Wiley online library; Scandinavian Journal of Immunology; March 17th 2022; Role of the antigen presentation process in the immunization mechanism of the genetic vaccines against COVID-19 and the need for biodistribution evaluations

McCullough, Peter Dr et al; Food and Chemical Toxicology; June 2022; Innate Immune Suppression by SARS-CoV-2 mRNA vaccinations: The role of G-quadruplexes, exosomes, and MicroRNAs;

Cole, Ryan; USA Watchdog; June 4th 2022; Global CV19 Vax Absolute Insanity

Cole, Ryan MD; June 6th 2022; Blood clot images raise concerns


## Chapter 10- Covid Vaccine Mandates

No College mandates; Substack; July 13th 2022; List of colleges and universities and their vaccine mandates;

---

Robb, David; Deadline; August 11th 2022; President Fran Drescher Calls For Review Of Hollywood's Covid Vaccination Mandate

Murtaugh, Isaiah; Ventura County Star; August 10th 2022; Days before classes start, vaccine mandate lifted at Ventura County community colleges

Shapiro, Nina; Seattle Times; Enrollment plummets at Washington Colleges; April 24th 2022

My Northwest; July 1, 2022; Gov. Inslee permanently mandates COVID-19 vaccines for WA agency employees

Markovich, Matt; Q-13 Fox; Gov. Inslee drops COVID booster mandate for WA state workers; (August 10th 2022)

Burdick, Suzanne, PhD; Children's Health Defense, October 20th 2022; 'Child Abuse on a Massive Scale': CDC Advisers Recommend Adding COVID Vaccines to Childhood Schedule

ABC7 New York; October 25th 2022; New York City appeals judge's ruling that could reinstate fired unvaccinated employees

Goldsberry, Jenny; Washington Examiner; October 9th 2022; Twitter reinstates Florida surgeon general's tweet after restricting it

Rantz, Jason; My Northwest; October 24th 2022; Rantz: AG Bob Ferguson is banning certain reporters from press conferences

## Chapter 11- A Letter from a Second Year Medical Student

Prasad, Vinay; Substack; July 29th 2022; A Medical Student's Thoughts During COVID-19: Crazy Policies

## Chapter 12 – The risk of dying from all causes vs the chance of a death involving Covid – All ages

OpenVAERS; Click on search reports, look to the left to fill out the field- select US only, Covid vaccine only, deceased "yes" write in age 0-30, click submit

Statistica; Resident population of the United States by sex and age as of July 1, 2021

CDC; Weekly Updates by Select Demographic and Geographic Characteristics; Sex and Age

**Rasmussen Reports; January 13th 2022;** COVID-19: Democratic Voters Support Harsh Measures Against Unvaccinated


## Chapter 13: Excess mortality in 25-44 year olds

Danish Health Authority; Vaccination against Covid-19 (Denmark's policies on Covid vaccination)

USMortality.com... There are many charts to see.


## Chapter 14: Excess Mortality: age 25-44

Mercola, Joseph MD; The Defender- Children's Health Defense; September 2nd 2022; What Is the Cause of Increased Mortality Rates?


## Chapter 15: Total number of deaths among 25-44 year olds: Comparing 2020 to 2021

Smally, Joe; Substack; September 4th 2022; Further evidence of mRNA injections associated with both COVID deaths and excess non-COVID deaths- Re-analysis of deaths of 18 to 55 year olds in the USA

Kirsch, Steve; Substack; September 12th 2022; Scientists from Harvard & Johns Hopkins Found Covid-19 Vaccines 98 Times Worse Than the Virus

## Chapter 16: Life insurance companies and the Funeral Business

Menge, Margaret; Substack; Crossroads Report; June 15th 2022; BREAKING: Fifth largest life insurance company in the US paid out 163% more for deaths of working people ages 18-64 in 2021 - Total claims/benefits up $6 BILLION

Wire Editor; Headline USA; January 3rd 2022; OneAmerica Insurance CEO: Deaths Increase 40% Among People Ages 18-64

J.Britt, Thomas FSA, MAAA; Correia, Paul FSA, MAAA; Hurley, Patrick FSA, MAAA; Krohn, Mike FSA, CERA, MAAA,et al; SOA Research Institute; August 2022; Group Life COVID-19 Mortality Survey Report

Berenson, Alex; Substack; Unreported Truths; August 5th 2022; The funeral business is doing great

Frei, Viva; Youtube Channel: Viva CLIPS!; video: Spike in "Sudden Adult Death Syndrome" (SADS) & Experts are BAFFLED as to WHY! Viva Clips (the comment was in response to the video.)

## Chapter 17- The highest vaccinated groups faces the 2021 Covid-related death wave

eugyppius: a plague chronicle; Substack; August 27th 2022; Exhaustive study of German mortality data finds excess deaths tightly correlated with mass vaccination

## Chapter 18- Covid vaccinations associated with injuries and deaths

Chudov, Igor; Substack; August 30th 2022; PROVEN RELATIONSHIP: COVID Boosters and Excess Mortality in 2022 - 29 Countries Show Strong Association between "Booster Uptake" and "Excess Mortality"

Notb-sports.org; The Wall; Sudden death and collapses within sports

## Chapter 19 -Attacks on Joe Rogan and alternative Covid treatments

Paterson, Alex; Media Matters; December 2nd 2021; Joe Rogan Wrapped: A year of COVID-19 misinformation, right-wing myths, and anti-trans rhetoric

Front Line COVID-19 Critical Care Alliance; Ivermectin in COVID-19

Kirsch, Steve; Substack; September 9th 2022; Why doctors aren't speaking out

The Palmer Foundation; May 30th 2021; Unprecedented Pandemic Turnaround in Uttar Pradesh with Dramatic Decline in Cases

Danish Health Authority; Vaccination against Covid-19

## Chapter 20- Discrimination against the unvaccinated

Desmet, Mattias; July 21, 2022; The Psychology of Totalitarianism

Kheriaty, Aaron; Brownstone Institute; December 14th 2021; Japan's Vaccination Policy: No Force, No Discrimination

Malone, Robert MD; Substack; September 7th 2022; The Continued Damages to our Children

Carlson, Tucker; Fox News; Tucker Carlson Tonight; October 5th 2022 (minute 20); https://www.youtube.com/watch?v=3tPAmjhMKHU&t=1369s


## Chapter 21: The pressure to vaccinate

Chapman, Jake; KIRO 7 News; August 11th 2022; Harborview Medical Center over 130% capacity

Ingraham, Christopher; The Washington Post; March 23rd 2020; Map: The places in America with the most (and fewest) ICU beds


## Chapter 22- The Vaccine Campaign: Using people of influence and Incentives

Durden, Tyler; Zerohedge; August 28th 2022; Rockefeller Foundation Wants Behavioral Scientists To Come Up With More Convincing COVID Vaxx Narratives

## Chapter 23- Mass Formation

Desmet, Mattias; 2022 book: The Psychology of Totalitarianism

Malone, Robert Dr; Substack; December 9th 2021; MASS FORMATION PSYCHOSIS or... mass hypnosis- the madness of crowds

Macius, Amanda; Business Insider; July 1st 2015; The lone German man who refused to give Hitler a Nazi salute

Alting von Geusau, Christiaan W.J.M; Brownstone Institute; November 17th 2021;Totalitarianism and the five stages of dehumanization

Harrington, Thomas; Brownstone Institute; July 6th 2022; How many among us are suckers?

Yeardon,Micheal MD; Doctors for Covid Ethics; April 10th 2022; The Covid Lies

Alexander, Paul, MD; Substack; September 9th 2022; New evidence uncovered in a lawsuit's discovery suggests the White House ordered the targeting-deplatforming-censoring of Dr. Naomi Wolf


## 24- Vaccine Injuries

Malone, Robert W, MD; Substack; August 2nd 2022; Data doesn't lie: mRNA-vaccines and correlation to all-cause mortality

Kirsch, Steve; Substack; August 25th 2022; Silenced healthcare workers speak out publicly for the first time

McCullough, Peter, MD; The McCullough Report; America Outloud; August 22, 2022; Spike Protein Drives Explosive Heart Inflammation in Teenagers

Madhava, Setty, MD; Children's Health Defense; August 16th 2022; CDC Quietly Removes 'Claim' That Spike Protein Doesn't 'Last Long' in Body After COVID Vaccine

Crispin-Miller, Mark; Substack; August 24th 2022; In memory of those who 'died suddenly,' in the United States, August 15-August 22

Hunter, Greg; USA Watchdog; August 13th 2022; "Hell No" to Any CV19 Vax – Lt. Col. Theresa Long MD

Geller, Pamela; The Geller Report; August 24th 2022; Whistleblower: Military Covers Up Alarming COVID Vaccination Side Effects

Greene, Shana; Newsweek; January 19 2021; Are Pharmaceutical Companies Immune From COVID-19 Vaccine Lawsuits?

Chudov, Igor; Substack; October 21$^{st}$ 2022; Cancer Rates are Increasing -- and May Get Much Worse - Wiped Out Immune Systems Take Time to Manifest

The Ethical Skeptic; August 30th 2022; Houston, We Have A Problem (Part 1 of 3)

Layton, Jeremy; November 1st 2022; Adam Zimmer, Bengals assistant coach, Dead at Age 38

## Chapter 25- The mainstream is awakening

Waleburger, Chris; Substack; September 15th 2022; Has the Depopulation Hypothesis Been Proven Correct? -Deaths Up, Births Down.

Chudov, Igor; Substack; September 15th 2022; POLITICO: How Bill Gates Took Over the Covid Pandemic - Bill Gates took over Covid just like he took over Operating Systems

Banco, Erin; Politico; September 14th 2022; How Bill Gates and partners used their clout to control the global Covid response — with little oversight

Bardosh, Kevin; Krug, Allison; Jamrozik, Euzebiusz, et al; SSRN; September 12th 2022; COVID-19 Vaccine Boosters for Young Adults: A Risk-Benefit Assessment and Five Ethical Arguments against Mandates at Universities

Turner, Michael, Dr; Substack; August 31st 2022; Losing My (Vaccine) Religion: A Doctor's Journey From Hope to Despair - A Tragic COVID Opera in 4 Acts

Greene, Jenna; Reuters; October 12th 2022; New data is out on COVID vaccine injury claims. What's to make of it?

**Conclusion-**

G. Edward Griffin's Need to Know; August 22nd 2022; Court Sides with 12-Year-Old Girl Refusing to Take Covid Vaccine Against Her Will

Malhotra, Assem, Dr; AOAIS publishing; Journal of Insulin Resistance; September 26th 2022; Curing the pandemic of misinformation on COVID-19 mRNA vaccines through real evidence-based medicine - Part 2

Kirsch, Steve; Substack; September 27th 2022; Top doctor who once promoted COVID vaccines on TV, now says they should be halted

Rogers, Toby; Substack; October 26th 2022; The Monstrous State of Things

Nevradakis, Michael, Ph.D; The Defender; October 26th 2022; Millions of Americans Were Assigned 'COVID-19 Violation' Scores Based on Cellphone Data Collected During Lockdowns